WOMEN
OF THE
STREET

WOMEN OF THE STREET

Making It on Wall Street–
The World's Toughest Business

Sue Herera

JOHN WILEY & SONS, INC.

New York • Chichester • Brisbane • Toronto • Singapore • Weinheim

Copyright © 1997 by Sue Herera

Published by John Wiley & Sons, Inc.

Text design by Tenenbaum Design

Illustrations by Ralph Bulter

Library of Congress Cataloging-in-Publication Data:

Herera, Sue, 1957–
    Women of the Street : making it on Wall Street—the world's
toughest business / Sue Herera.
        p.   cm.
    Includes index.
    ISBN 0-471-15331-1 (cloth : alk. paper)
    1. Women stockbrokers—United States—Biography.   2. Wall Street.
I. Title.
HG4621.H47   1996
332.64'092'273—dc20
    [B]   96–34284

Printed in the United States of America

10 9 8 7 6 5 4 3 2 1

To all the women of the Street,

past, present, and future.

And, to Dan for all his love and support.

CONTENTS

THE INTERVIEWS

Mary Farrell   1

Managing Director, PaineWebber. *Mary Farrell readily admits to having made huge personal sacrifices for her career. Her devotion to the Street meant timing the birth of her daughter in between earnings seasons—so she could be available to her clients. Her climb to the top has been peppered with numerous battles against sexism, but it's paid off. She is one of the most respected and visible women in her field: a savvy market maven and a prominent media figure.*

Bridget Macaskill   15

President and CEO, Oppenheimer Funds. *Next time you have a glass of orange juice, think of Bridget Macaskill. Now one of the most prominent women on the Street, she got her start in Great Britain helping a food company market orange juice. After relocating to the United States with her husband so he could pursue a career in the financial services industry, she was hired by Oppenheimer to help them market their financial products in Great Britain. She knew nothing about Wall Street or the financial services business at the time, but she knew how to package products and sell them. Using the old orange juice theory, she's risen to the top at Oppenheimer and managed to balance a demanding career with what she describes as the most important thing in her life: her family. The key to success, she claims, is to become an expert "juggler."*

tion of the markets, Liz was studying Russian in high school. Her "big picture" approach has served her well professionally, helping her to establish a large international clientele. She works nonstop and spends nearly all her free time reading as much as she can on the industries she covers. Liz claims that her work ethic and broad knowledge base—in addition to a very good sense of humor—are the secrets to her success.

Muriel Siebert   83

Muriel Siebert & Co. Known as the First Lady of Wall Street, Muriel is perhaps the most frequently interviewed woman on the Street. Truly a trailblazer for women in the business, she was the first woman to own a seat on the New York Stock Exchange—no small feat at the time, as 9 out of 10 men she asked to sponsor her declined. Muriel was also the first female bank regulator for the state of New York. She now runs her own discount brokerage with approximately 80,000 retail accounts. Hands down, Muriel is the most dynamic and colorful woman on the Street.

Gail M. Dudack   99

Managing Director and Chief Investment Strategist, UBS Securities, LLC. Gail Dudack never really intended to have a career. She thought she'd have four kids and settle down in a nice house with a white picket fence. But then came a summer job on Wall Street that changed her life forever. Gail found her niche in technical analysis, and at the tender age of 25 appeared on Wall $treet Week *with* Louis Rukeyser. *Gail is also a founding member of the International Federation of Technical Analysts and a member and former president of the Market Technicians Association—the two dominant (and overwhelmingly male) professional societies for technical analysts.*

Grace Fey   115

Executive Vice President and Director, Frontier Capital Management. As the manager responsible for $300 million under management and 200 clients, Grace Fey heads Frontier Capital Management's high net worth and small institutional client accounts. She began her career in 1970 at Alliance Capital Management and worked as a general analyst at United Business Service (the publisher of the United Business Review*) and as a portfolio manager at Keystone Investment Management Corporation. She also helped build two small independent management firms in the Boston area. Grace is a Chartered Financial Analyst (CFA)* *and has been featured in* Business Week, USA Today, *the* Wall Street Journal, Wall Street Transcript, Financial Planning, *and* Changing Times.

President and CEO, Maria Fiorini Ramirez Capital, Inc. Maria Fiorini Ramirez is a self-described matchmaker, although not in the traditional sense of the phrase. She claims that one of the most important things she does is bring people together, whether clients or friends, to create a truly global network of contacts and sources. It is this network that helps keep her in touch with what's happening around the world and helps her manage money so successfully. Maria started on the Street in 1968 with American Express International Banking Corporation and has also served as vice president and senior money market economist at Merrill Lynch, and managing director and money market economist at Drexel Burnham Lambert. When Drexel fell, Maria struck out on her own and now runs a $40 million global advisory firm. She's one of the most visible women on the Street and appears frequently on CNBC, CNN, the pages of the Wall Street Journal, *and the Dow Jones advisory service.*

Chief Technical Analyst, Kimelman & Baird, LLC. When Bernadette first started on Wall Street, they were still using tote boards to record trades. One day in the 1950s, she noticed that everyone around her was selling except her boss—who, using technical analysis, was finding points to successfully buy the market. The experience changed her approach to the markets forever, and she is now known affectionately as the "queen of the charts." Bernadette was the first woman to head the Market Technicians Association and the New York Society of Technical Analysts. She also makes time for extensive charity work, donating her financial expertise to several religious organizations.

President and CEO, Garzarelli Investment Management. Elaine is best known as the analyst who called the 1987 stock market crash and subsequent bull market run on national TV, forever earning her the title "market guru." To this day, when Elaine talks, Wall Street listens. She routinely moves markets with her predictions and, by her own admission, is not afraid to stick her neck out. Elaine credits her success to her over-

whelming devotion to her work, which she also says has eliminated any chance at living a "normal" life. In fact, Elaine's devotion to the markets started very early in her professional life. She designed her own economic model as an intern at Drexel Burnham Lambert and has built on that model for much of her career. Elaine is formerly the chief market strategist at Lehman Brothers, and she now heads her own firm in New York City. Elaine eschews the traditional office setting—too distracting—and instead prefers the quiet of home. The big Wall Street firms have more than doubled her research assistants' salaries in an effort to lure them away from Elaine and learn the secrets to her success.

LBR Group. Linda is considered by many to be one of the top traders in the world, profiled in the best-selling New Market Wizards by Jack Schwager. She began her career as an options trader on the Pacific Stock Exchange—a competitive world populated mostly by men. Linda has an uncanny ability to tune out background noise and just focus on the markets. She overcame numerous obstacles on her road to success, including a three-year bout with chronic fatigue syndrome, during which she felt she would be relieved to die. Her keen sense of focus and determination helped her recover and take on life and the markets with a new perspective.

Senior Investment Management Consultant, Smith Barney. By all accounts it was highly unlikely that Julie Stone would end up with a career on the Street. A young mother and divorcee, she didn't understand traditional finance. But, her mother had taught her some important cash management techniques by keeping money in little envelopes for household expenses. It was this basic and intuitive approach to money and the desire to provide for her child that eventually brought Julie to a new career as a broker for a major NYSE firm. She is now a leader in investment management consulting and has more than $100 million under her watch. Julie is among the top investment management consultants at Smith Barney.

PREFACE

In the 16 years I've been covering Wall Street, I've seen increasingly more women take an interest in the financial markets. It really wasn't all that long ago that playing the markets was considered the domain of men, and to a large extent, the media reflected this bias. When I started at FNN back in 1981, however, I could see that was about to change. In the past very few women worked in business news, but FNN was comprised of at least 50 percent women, with several anchoring newscasts. In traditional network news, women had already shattered the glass ceiling and spread across the airwaves: Jane Pauley, Andrea Mitchell, Leslie Stahl, Jessica Savitch, to name just a few, and, of course, Barbara Walters. In those early days on FNN it seemed the business media was about to play catch-up.

As the fabric of our society has changed, so too have the financial markets. Today, as many women as men are investing in the markets. Women watch their investments shrewdly, learn as much as they can about the markets, and try to make educated, informed financial decisions—just as their male counterparts do. Over the years, I have had the privilege of hearing from many CNBC viewers. Female viewers, especially, have shared their successes and failures in the markets with me. For every success story I've heard, there has been an accompanying tale of frustration, some vaguely reminiscent of the kind of condescension and discrimination women are sometimes subjected to in car dealerships: Brokers don't listen to their questions or take them seriously. Most of the professional expertise women must turn to for guidance is dispensed by men; the markets seem like a male game and the men who control the game board don't seem eager to explain the rules. Thus, my first inclination when considering a book project was to write about the differences that women face in investing.

However, upon reflection, it seemed a rather silly idea: A stock is a stock, a bond a bond, and price/earnings ratios and T-bill rates are the same for men as for women. In fact, it occurred to me that a book specially targeting female investors could be downright condescending. Men don't have some special genetic coding that makes them better fit for playing the markets. It's simply a matter of education and knowledge. Once you understand how it works, it's really quite simple (or equally as difficult). Virtually all the information one needs to learn about the markets can be found on the newsstand and on bookstore shelves across the country. A book on investing for women would not be a meaningful addition to the current literature.

But what got me thinking were the comments "that most of the finance and investment professionals are men." This statement stuck in my mind: Wait a minute, I thought, that's simply not true. Over the years, and especially recently, I've interviewed many highly placed female investment professionals who are managing hundreds of millions of dollars. From analysts to fund managers and traders, women have firmly established themselves on the Street—they've made their mark. So why is it that they are still not popularly perceived to have the same stature and success as their male counterparts? That was the impetus for this book.

Women of the Street is a look at the ladies who shape the markets: where they came from, how they got where they are, and who they are as people. In my decade and a half of reporting on the financial markets, I have interviewed many of the top women in finance. Liz

Bramwell, Elaine Garzarelli, Muriel Siebert, and the other women you will meet in the following pages have made no less a contribution to the marketplace than the Jeff Viniks and Peter Lynches. However, the ascension of these women to the hallowed halls of Wall Street has been a different journey than that experienced by the Jim Rogers, Jim Grants, and other men who grace the pages of the financial press on a daily basis.

And while I could probably tell you where these women stood on the issue of real interest rates or the direction of the stock market, I found I didn't really *know* them at all. I've felt a kinship with them, simply because I'm a woman covering Wall Street and the Street has always been a predominantly male enclave. But while I know that you and I are interested in their take on the markets, I thought it time for us to get to know them a bit better on a personal level: to hear how they came to choose their profession, many of them at a time when there were no female role models; to learn how they rose to levels of prominence and influence; to share in their success and failures; and to gain some insight into their personal and professional struggles, past and present.

I am both grateful and flattered that the "Women of the Street" trusted me enough to tell me about their climb to the top. I hope that you will find their stories as inspirational and informative as I did. Whether you are an investor, a seasoned financial professional, or an aspiring market player, these interviews should provide you with new insight—insight that will either inspire you to new heights or have you running as far as possible from the Street.

ACKNOWLEDGMENTS

This book is very much a labor of love. It is the combined efforts of several very talented and dedicated people. Special thanks to my editor and friend, Pamela van Giessen, who has thrown her heart and soul into the project. This book is as much hers as it is mine.

Women of the Street would not even exist if Mark Etzkorn hadn't come on board midstream. I cannot thank him enough for putting his life on hold to take on this project. His insightful writing and his exceptional commitment to the book have been a godsend.

Larry Chambers deserves a special thanks for helping to get this project off the ground.

Many thanks to my friend and producer, Richard Fisherman. His encouragement and support helped get me through the rough spots, and his critical eye was invaluable.

And, to John Murphy, a special thank you for urging me to undertake this project and for always being there with a kind word and a little bit of Irish luck, too.

INTRODUCTION

Since the advent of women's liberation in the 1960s, the media has regularly lavished attention on various women's issues: From the bedroom to the boardroom, we have been inundated with books, magazine articles, reports, and television shows on the uniqueness of the female experience—how life is different for women at work and at play than it is for men. *Men Are from Mars* and *You Just Don't Understand* focused on communication differences, *The Hite Report* on sexual differences, and *The Glass Ceiling* on career differences. This trend shows no signs of reversing: 1996 brought us *Divided Lives,* a chronicle of the successes and failures of three prominent women—a journalist, a conductor, and a surgeon—struggling to balance and integrate their personal and professional selves.

A common theme running throughout many books of this type is how women define themselves and overcome challenges in a world where men, in many ways, still make most of the rules: handling the condescension or outright discrimination in the workplace; the desire to fulfill more "traditional" goals of family life without guilt and without fearing criticism from other career-oriented women; and the difficulty in reconciling these often conflicting aspirations.

Nowhere are these themes played out with greater vigor and clarity than in the high-rolling, high-pressured world of Wall Street, which has traditionally filled the role of America's ultimate men's club. This is precisely why a look into the lives of the women who came, saw, and conquered in this world is the quintessential commentary on what it's like for a woman to make it in a man's world. While women can point to significant inroads in almost every area of U.S. business, political, and cultural life over the last 30 years, the trading rooms and offices of the Street have been more resistant to change than many other industries and professions. Nowhere are the lines between the sexes drawn more clearly than in the crisscrossing avenues of money and power in lower Manhattan.

Wall Street has long been, in both myth and reality, a world populated by swaggering men. From the Seligmans to the Morgans, from the Rockefellers to the Buffets, the investment marketplace of yesterday and today has long been portrayed by the press as the province of brash white men in white shirts, tailored suits, and power ties who make and lose fortunes. Whether brilliant, lucky, brave, foolish, stubborn, or stupid, these men have captured the imagination of novelists and movie producers, as well as the financial press that covers them daily.

We seem to have an insatiable curiosity about the personalities who make names for themselves in this rough-and-tumble playground. From *Reminiscences of a Stock Operator* to more recent tomes on George Soros and Warren Buffet, many books have been published over the years about the *men* behind the money, all eagerly devoured by a public hungry for investment insights.

Women, it would appear from the majority of books published to date, do not play on the Street. Perhaps they do not receive a comparable degree of media attention because the financial press, like the industry it covers, has traditionally been dominated by men; and men, maybe, are more comfortable sharing their war stories with one of their own.

In 1996, however, the press that covers the Street is changing drastically. Louis Rukeyser, Lou Dobbs, and Marshall Loeb are no longer the only financial journalists on this beat. CNN and PBS now take a backseat to CNBC, Bloomberg, and a new gallery of names and faces—the faces of women. Connie Bruck and Carol Loomis, to name two, are the new players on this stage—and they are quite popular. Not surprisingly, when they beat the Street for a story, they often look to the women who have been quietly working their way up the ranks, making and losing fortunes with the best of their male counterparts. The stories you will read in this book will forever dispel the notion that the Street is only for the boys.

Some of the top woman traders, analysts, brokers, fund managers, and financial advisors share their personal stories and professional secrets to success. From the glamorous to the studious, readers will meet the "celebrities" who have heretofore merely brushed the front pages with their presence. But these women play second fiddle to no one. Highly successful by any standards—regardless of gender—they are true champions with compelling stories to tell and lessons to teach us about themselves, the often misunderstood world in which they work, and our society as a whole.

These are not the only women working on Wall Street, nor are they the only ones making a comfortable living there. At least in terms of raw numbers, women have significantly altered the sexual composition of the offices, war rooms, and trading floors of the financial industry over the past two decades. But only a relative handful can rightly be called "stars" in their field by virtue of their undeniable track records, their longevity, and the respect they've earned among their peers—both male and female. These are the select few who open up on the following pages.

And the list could have been longer: A few women—some who handle staggering amounts of money and wield incredible influence in the markets—chose not to speak out, for personal or professional reasons. Hopefully at some point in the future, we may hear the stories of these women, perhaps when books by and about successful female investment professionals and traders are more the rule than the exception.

Certain surprising facts emerged as I researched and interviewed different women on the Street. There are still hardly any female traders—pure traders—the stature of a George Soros, a Richard Dennis, a Paul Tudor Jones. Only two traders are profiled in this book. Female analysts and trade strategists seem to be more prevalent than female traders, perhaps because analysis showcases women's strengths: performing detailed, conscientious, consistent work, communicating it effectively, and connecting on a personal level with their clients and associates. It also may be because the research room was easier to break into than the trading room when these women were first forcing open doors on Wall Street; maybe women posed less of a threat there. And female mutual fund managers, although their numbers have increased dramatically in the last 10 years, still work in relative anonymity compared to some of their celebrated male counterparts.

The same holds true for hedge fund managers. Again, while women have made advances into this area, their presence is generally offshore and quiet. Peruse the bookshelves: Almost all the trading and investment books are penned by men. For the most part, women on Wall Street seem to make up an increasingly large, powerful, but still low-key subculture. We really have only just joined the battle here.

I found it fascinating to discover the similarities and differences in how these women each deal with the obstacles confronting them, not the least of which is maintaining their identities as women (and individuals) in an environment that often seems intent on judging female traits as handicaps or exploitable weaknesses. Unlike high-profile women in other professions who have spoken out loud and long about the discrimination they have experienced, most of these women exhibited a stoicism that was somewhat surprising.

Or maybe it's not. While they all acknowledged things like pay differences and social slights, they tended to downplay the significance of such barriers, perhaps in fear of appearing weak in a world where only the strong survive, or perhaps because a certain measure of pride might be taken in not letting them know they ever "got" to you. Only one woman, in fact, openly acknowledged blatant sexual discrimination on the Street. On the other hand, perhaps these women simply took the rules of the playground they entered at face value and accepted its demands as the price of pursuing their individual dreams. They're fighters, not whiners.

They have to be, given the nature of their business. "What have you done for me lately" is the name of the game, and today's hotshots become tomorrow's has-beens in the blink of an eye. There's always somebody waiting to put in longer hours, make the bold call, push the envelope.

As a result, taking a few months off for maternity leave or to spend more time with your family is, for the most part, not a viable option. It was a little depressing to hear how many of these women say they don't think they have "normal" lives. Extended hours, solitary work, and preempted social lives and outside interests are more common than not. Some of them do have families and say their success would not have been possible without the support and understanding of their spouses—but even then the challenge is extreme. The lengths they take to weather such adversity—and the sacrifices they must make—offer a sobering portrait of an industry that draws thousands every year with tantalizing whispers of excitement and affluence. Listen to Gail Dudack's admission that she always felt underpaid, but accepted lower salaries in exchange for a measure of security. And while you may at first envy Elaine Garzarelli for being able to work out of her home, you might reassess the glamour of high finance when you realize she made the switch just to give herself *more* time to devote exclusively to work.

Along with the demanding pace comes a great deal of isolation from co-workers, friends, families, and at times, the outside world in general; repeated references to long hours *alone* in an office, staring at a computer terminal or list of figures, abound. Linda Bradford Raschke, for example, recounts her "hermitlike" existence in an office with no windows. Mary Farrell jokingly describes a "close friend" she talks to twice a year, and says her own daughter is turned off by the amount of work she has to do. There is a price to pay for the privilege of breathing the rarefied air in top positions on the Street. But for the most part, these women wouldn't have it any other way.

One lesson may be that there's still a long way to go. While women have managed to minimize, ignore, or overcome obstacles on the Street, the very nature of the business makes it an ongoing battle, and some women still might not feel at liberty to call a spade a spade. There are probably more than a few "old-timers" (or newcomers who have inherited their mind-set) who still believe women can't cut it on the Street and are waiting for them to pack it in and head back to the kitchen. It may be many more years before the seeds these women planted in the industry bear fruit.

What crystallized for me, though, throughout the course of these interviews, was the sense of a shared value system and approach to business that sets these women apart from the men in their field. Money and power go hand in hand on Wall Street, and men connect the two automatically—they often appear to care less about what people think of them and focus exclusively on the money as the ultimate goal.

The women in these pages certainly don't disdain the money that comes with success on the Street, but they seem more fulfilled by the idea that they're helping and empowering their clients: A sense of satisfaction with what they do and a feeling that they are valued and respected for consistent quality work seems to take precedence over instant notoriety and a quick killing in the markets.

While these woman have only recently begun to attract the same media attention as men on the Street, many of them have been steadily building their reputations and businesses for three decades and stress the importance of being around for the long haul.

To men in the business, it may seem superfluous or even incongruous that these women almost all view themselves as "nice people" and consider it important that others do as well—especially clients. They make an effort to be responsive, focus on customer needs, and avoid the hard sell. In doing so, surprisingly, they have been able to transform such typically frowned upon "feminine" characteristics into a business advantage. The combination of personal warmth and a strong work ethic is an attractive attribute to other professionals (especially women) who are quick enough to realize, as Elizabeth Mackay pointed out in her interview, that women have to work twice as hard and be twice as smart to make the same impression as men. In that light, who would you rather have handle your money?

However, this may explain why, despite their undeniable bottom-line performance, these women still lag behind the George Soroses, Warren Buffets, and even the Michael Milkens of the investment world in terms of publicity. The other element of the Wall Street money/power equation is ego, and men still outflank women at the game of attracting attention to themselves—regardless of whether the attention is scathing criticism or lavish praise. Either way, men seem gratified by the ego boost and will go to great lengths to fill this need. By contrast, women are more focused on their reputations and what people think of them as individuals— good publicity is the only kind they're interested in. The temptation to become a Soros is outweighed by the fear of being perceived a Milken or a Boesky.

Ironically, by concentrating on nurturing their professional skills and building respectable careers in relative anonymity, they have not capitalized to the same extent as men on the influence that is one of the side benefits of a heightened public profile. It's similar to what Muriel Siebert mentions in her interview: Women have amassed a great deal of real, tangible power in the business world, but they haven't learned to leverage it the same way men have—to maximize its effectiveness and expand their sphere of influence.

The interviews compiled here are a mosaic of sorts. Each one is unique, with it's own distinct color and importance, to be appreciated for its individual qualities; together though, the pieces form a complete mural, the unfolding story of the ascension of women in one of the last bastions of male dominance—the Street.

WOMEN
OF THE
STREET

Mary Farrell

Managing Director, PaineWebber

Making a name for yourself in any field requires dedication, passion, and of course, a little bit of luck. In the notoriously competitive world of Wall Street, persistence and drive are absolute necessities if you're going to survive the ups and downs that come with the territory. Not surprisingly, the business is rife with Type-A personalities, that oft-maligned group of goal-setters and go-getters who vie to put in the longest hours, turn in the most reports, make the most commissions, or manage the most money. Just as predictably, the burnout rate in the industry is staggering. Many are lured by the Street's siren song, but few survive years of trench warfare with their balance sheets, reputations, and sanity intact. It takes a special breed to stick it out and prosper.

Walking through midtown Manhattan on a brisk January day, clutching a cappuccino in my freezing hands as I looked for Paine-Webber's headquarters, I was on my way to meet just such a person: a woman of legendary work habits, a driven market maven respected both by her industry peers and the business media. Mary Farrell, managing director at PaineWebber, is a well-known commentator on the Street and a regular on *Wall Street Week with Louis Rukeyser.*

Any woman who wants to work on the Street will benefit from Mary's story. Relaxed, candid, and assertive, she pulls no punches. To get an idea of what it takes to make it on the Street—and make it there as a woman—talk to Mary Farrell.

Mary's office was on the ninth floor, the same floor as the trading room. As she escorted me down the hall, the noise grew increasingly loud and intense. "After a while, you don't even hear it," she said, and continued on. The first thing I noticed when I entered her private office was a huge black chair in the corner, looming like a medieval torture device, complete with pulleys and ropes. I stopped in my tracks and stared. "Don't worry, it won't bite you!" Mary laughed, catching my reaction. "I don't have time to go to the gym and work out, so I work out on that machine."

Even though Mary was an economics major at Manhattanville College, a career on the Street was apparently not her first option—or her second or third to hear her tell it. "Embarrassingly," she said, laughing slightly, "I'd gone to college in the 1960s, which was, of course, the 'revolution,' so the last thing I wanted to do was go to Wall Street." But after she graduated, she went to New York, and needing money, answered an ad in the *New York Times* for an "economics major for a securities analyst trainee." "I didn't know what a securities analyst was," Mary admitted, "but I did have the economics major. I was so naive about New York that I thought the address I sent the resume to, 120 Broadway, had something to do with the theater. I knew nothing. The placement office at my college certainly wasn't directing women to jobs. They assumed women would get married after graduation. Anyway, I answered the ad and realized at the interview that this was something I really wanted to do."

It was at Pershing & Company (now part of Donaldson, Lufkin Jenrette) that Mary got her start. But when she realized she'd need an advanced degree to get ahead in the business, she immediately enrolled in night school and earned her MBA from the Stern School of Business at NYU. Anyone on the Street will tell you that what Mary wants, Mary eventually gets.

When Mary entered Wall Street in the early 1970s, women were a relative rarity, at least in nonclerical positions. I asked her what it was like in those days. Mary replied, "Well, I have an interesting slant on the Street in that I respect its realism. The director of research at Pershing would hire a woman college graduate every year to train as an analyst; even he acknowledged he could get talent cheaper by hiring women. But I didn't care at the time, it was an opening. Back in 1971, job training that led to a professional position was very hard to find."

The women working on Wall Street in the '70s were essentially trailblazers for women on the Street today. Mary minced no words about the challenges she faced early on. "I found it extremely difficult. I was absolutely amazed at how hard it was, that there was so little support. There was never a sense that you would be taken seriously. There was blatant discrimination. To get ahead, you did have to be twice as good and work twice as hard. Nobody was going to give you a promotion easily. You had to fight for it. It was also not unusual to find yourself being paid half of what the equivalent male analysts were getting. Directors of research had the attitude that as a woman you should just be grateful you had the job at all. I was a budding feminist and the injustice of it all infuriated me. So I developed an 'I'll show them' attitude. I'm always amazed when I read statements like, 'Women—why train them? They don't stay long enough.' "

As she remembered the slights she and other women had to endure, it didn't seem as if Mary's sarcasm about such treatment had diminished with the passing of time. "There was frequent job chang-ing by women in the '70s, but look at what our options were: Should I smash my head against this brick wall, or try another com-pany where I may not have to face this kind of discrimination? I changed jobs three times before I landed at Merrill Lynch, which was the first firm that really gave women equal opportunity. My boss in the research department at Merrill didn't care whether you were male, female, purple, green, or what, as long as your stocks went up. That was really the first time I felt I got a fair shake."

Most of the women I've interviewed, I told Mary, said that what they like about this business is that it's a bottom-line industry—if you can get in the right area, and prove your performance, it's almost gender neutral. Mary shared her thoughts. "I think that's why, espe-cially in the '70s and '80s, women like myself gravitated to research or sales positions," Mary said. "There is an objective bottom line in those areas. I still think, even in the '90s, that women who go into corporate finance are asking for trouble. That environment is ram-pant with discrimination against women, and judgment remains highly subjective. It's easier to prove yourself in research and sales. Fortunately, Wall Street got enlightened by the '80s and '90s and figured out women weren't going to go away, so the environment changed very positively."

Anyone who doubts that Mary Farrell is one of the most dedi-cated money managers on the Street would be well advised to con-sider the circumstances under which she gave birth to her two chil-dren. "When I had children, I tried to time them so they didn't come when earnings were being reported," Mary explained simply. "Peo-ple had bet money on my judgment and I would never abandon them—I felt an intense personal sense of responsibility. I think that's why I have such good relationships with clients today. They under-stand that they won't be abandoned for any reason, just as I would never abandon my kids."

Mary acknowledged that while Wall Street has gotten much better about professional women having children, she is surprised (and a little put off) that a sense of entitlement exists among some women—especially the younger generation for whom she and her contemporaries knocked down barriers. "I think some of the younger women today view it as, 'I may have a professional position, but I'm entitled to my three month maternity leave. For those three months, I'm out of here,'" Mary said, laughing wryly. "I just could never have done that because I felt such a strong commitment to my clients. I find that there is somewhat of a generation gap in that respect. Something that bridges this, though, is the effort to allow women to job share. I think that kind of creative solution is much better for women and their clients. When you're a new mother, it doesn't make sense to kill yourself working as hard as before, but you don't want to lose your clients either. It's a very hard choice, and you have to find creative solutions. At the time I had children, I felt if I took any time off, I would never get back in and my career would be over. But that wasn't necessarily true. I could have been more relaxed about it all. But when you're going through it, it isn't that easy."

Mary nodded and, raising an eyebrow, added cynically, "Yes, I definitely felt pressure. I have a friend who was one of the first women analysts on the Street, and a good one. When she left to have her child, she told management she was coming back. But when she returned, they'd given her office away. They stuck her in a tiny closet space because they didn't think she'd stay long. That was the kind of thing we had to contend with in those days, and the law didn't back women up then. We were subject to the whims of management."

I pulled my chair closer to her desk. How do you balance such a demanding career with a family? I asked. "Well, I was helped by one important thing: I actually came to PaineWebber because the director of research was a woman with two children," Mary replied, "and I wanted to have a second child. She accommodated me by letting me out of travel when my children were young. I think if more firms were more accommodating and looked at it as a long-term investment, it would be better for everybody.

"Also," Mary continued, "I had a working mother, so I think I was much more realistic about what could be done. Growing up in that environment, I understood very clearly that it's better to have a job that pays more rather than less, because you can buy services that will make your life easier. My sister is a social worker. It took her two years to get a degree in social work and two more years to get an MBA. When she returned to the workforce, social work didn't pay enough to pay a regular baby-sitter. I was much more realistic. I figured that if you're going to be a working mother, it's nice to come home to a clean apartment, with dinner cooked and the kids taken care of. I learned from my mother early that when you have children, your time is not your own. You just don't have the options you used to. If you love to browse in antiques stores, or whatever, you can't do it much anymore. You're not able to go to the spa, or just take off for a romantic vacation. Your life is with your children. Your social life changes and you don't throw sophisticated dinner parties. You do family-oriented things, like having picnics with other working parents and their kids, because you all want to socialize with your children."

She summed the matter up. "It hasn't been easy, and I understand why women may take another road. Even my own daughter said, 'I don't want to do what you did. I don't want to work that hard.' It makes me feel kind of sad because she only perceives the negative side of it. On the other hand, it will be very telling to see what she actually does, as opposed to what she says she's going to do." Mary paused, turning the matter over in her mind. "I'm realistic," she continued. "I want to convey to my daughter that it's a fact that 50 percent of marriages end in divorce, so she'd better be prepared to support herself and possibly her children. When I was in college, I was told, 'Get your teaching degree in case, God forbid, you should ever have to support yourself.' Teaching was something a woman could fall back on if she were widowed or something ill-fated happened. I've seen too many of my contemporaries who weren't prepared left out in the cold in very unpleasant circumstances, trying to pull things together in their 30s and 40s."

Ironically, Mary has to rein in her daughter sometimes when it comes to overworking. "I want my children to have choices I didn't have, but I'm always telling my teenage daughter not to work so hard. She's on the track team and the cross country team. She practices five days a week and every weekend. Two of her five courses are advanced placement. I tell her, 'Honey, high school is a time to enjoy yourself. Why are you signing up for advanced courses? Why don't you take it easy? You're too busy.' I tell her to relax and have fun because there will be time to work hard later.

"My own mother worked out of choice to send her children to college. It wasn't that she wanted a career, but I saw that she was actually happier than many of her housewife friends because she got up and went to work every day. Then Betty Friedan's *The Feminine Mystique* came out, about all the housewives living in the suburbs who were supposed to be happy but were actually miserable. My mother probably felt some conflict because women then weren't supposed to work, but it gave her an outlet that she was actually very happy with. When her kids went off to college, she still had her job. She was ready to retire when she hit her 60s, but working definitely had a positive impact on her."

I ventured to ask why she thought she was so successful. She immediately replied. "Persistence. I remember reading once that the most important attribute of successful people is not that they always succeed, but that they respond to failure by coming back and redoubling their efforts. I came from a family where we were all able to get scholarships to go to college, and we all started working early to save money for college. We got the message that you have to do it yourself. It's up to you. It's your choice. We were all activists about getting what we wanted and all have at least one graduate degree. So I just applied that resolve to Wall Street. The difference was that I was shocked at how tough Wall Street was; there were so many obstacles. I was motivated to work hard, but instead of somebody saying, 'Boy, are we lucky to have this woman,' I had to constantly prove myself. It was just absolute persistence that got me through it, and refusing to take 'no' for an answer."

She's learned to be philosophical about the challenges she had to confront in the '70s as a woman in the business. "The biggest affront was not being taken seriously," she remembered. "Sometimes I was the only woman in the department, and there were certain painful incidents. For instance, companies would hold meetings in clubs that didn't allow women. They wouldn't even think of it, and then when I'd arrive, everyone would be embarrassed, and I would get cut out of the meeting. Sometimes firms would have social outings at private golf clubs that only allowed men. But by far, the worst show of disrespect was that women were not paid as much as men. I asked very simply to be paid what the men were paid. I became obsessed that management would not be able to find me lacking in even one single measurement—whatever they measured. Whether it was number of pages written, stock price performance, client contact, whatever. I'd find out what the numbers were, and I'd make sure I was in the top ten percent or top quarter on every single measure." Mary shook her head slowly. "But they would still not pay me equally, and wouldn't think anything of it. Sometimes I wonder why I didn't give up—it was so frustrating at times—but I'm glad I never did, because the '80s and '90s have been such a wonderful period on Wall Street for women with enormous opportunity. It's been one of the best places in the world for a woman to have a career."

I commented that Mary actually seemed to thrive on the challenge of proving herself in a man's world. Nodding her head in agreement, Mary said, "Yes, I was very determined that I would win. They could do all that, but I was going to win in the end. Building outside visibility became part of my strategy in the early days. If management didn't recognize my worth inside the firm, then I would build credibility outside, so they would be forced to face it. I remember once speaking on a panel of managing directors and senior vice presidents, and my title was that of assistant vice president. I circled my title on the program and sent it to my boss, with a note, 'This is embarrassing. This is my peer group.' In a perfect world, I wouldn't have had to do that. I did get a promotion shortly after that, which I felt was long overdue. Being a panelist on *Wall $treet Week with Louis Rukeyser* has been a tremendous experience, and the exposure very positive for my career."

Given the discrimination Mary saw in her immediate workplace early on, I wondered how she was able to go about building a successful reputation on Wall Street as a whole. She answered, "It was not as difficult as I thought it would be, partly because I love people—it sounds like such a corny thing, such a 'woman's thing'—but I genuinely do, and I've always enjoyed working with clients. However, I hate the whole concept of women 'networking.' I often get calls from strangers: 'Can we have lunch?' I don't even have time to have lunch with my closest friends. I don't feel like having lunch and giving advice to a stranger, just because we both happen to be women. Or a woman will call up to enlist my help in getting her a job, but I save those chips for people who are close to me. If I'm going to recommend somebody, it's got to be somebody I know and trust, not a stranger. I did join the Financial Women's Association early; I've been very active on the board and I enjoy that organization. I have made many important contacts there and genuine friends. Contrary to what you might read, there really was an incredible sense of helping other women in the '70s and even today."

I found this ironic, because I'd heard from some women that there isn't the same camaraderie among women today on Wall Street that there is among men—that there's so much competition, they can't afford it. According to Mary, men have an advantage in this respect. "Women, especially working mothers, don't tend to go into a bar every Friday night and have a couple of beers with their peers. We go home to our kids. I think women simply have less time to socialize. On the other hand, our bonds are very strong. My friend, Denise, another professional working mother, joked with someone the other day, 'Mary is my best friend. We talk twice a year and actually see each other once a year.' We've been friends for over 20 years, and when the kids have moved on, we know we'll see much more of each other. So, yes, I think women are more limited in how they can spend their time, but on the other hand, there is a very strong bond among women."

Her reputation on the Street firmly established, Mary spoke proudly of her progress, both personal and professional, and remembered a time when she wasn't that sure of herself—a turning point in her career. "I was going to interview for a job I really wanted at Merrill Lynch in 1978. They had started a prestigious emerging growth stock group. One of the members of the Financial Women's Association had said to the head of the Merrill group, 'You ought to interview Mary Farrell. She does emerging growth at Smith Barney.' I was having lunch with a friend before the interview and confessed, 'Oh, I'm so nervous. I really want this job, but they're looking for someone with more seniority and reputation. I don't think I'm going to be able to pull this off.' She turned to me and said, 'Mary, do you realize that if you were a man you'd be telling me how good you are, that you have a great record, that you have already established loyal clients, and how you can be a major player in this group. You'd not only be telling me that—you'd be believing it. But instead, because you're a woman, you're considering your deficiencies and where you don't measure up. You're worrying that you've only worked x number of years, instead of a few more. You have to think like a man, that you're great, that you have a lot to offer, and not what your deficiencies are.' That was a big turning point for me psychologically, even though it doesn't sound like a big deal, because it was the first time I ever thought in those terms. All those years of being underpaid, directors not giving me a fair shake, whatever, had left me professionally feeling like I had some shortcoming. I remember preparing for the interview and really taking a very different tack—offering myself in a convincing and positive way. When you're a victim of a stereotype, you can start incorporating those qualities into your psyche. Merrill was another important turning point, because it was the first place I was treated fairly."

Mary's longevity and success puts her in a prime position to comment on the advantages and disadvantages of being a woman on Wall Street. As she observed, "I really don't think women and men are all that different. I didn't decide to major in economics and get that MBA in order to compete with men. I dropped out of art history in college for instance, just because I thought it was boring. If you're in this kind of a job, you've probably gravitated here because your skills are in this direction, whether you're male or female. I think the obvious disadvantages were factors in the '70s, but diminished markedly in the '80s, and are rare in the '90s.

"Sometimes I think women have a certain advantage. I have seen women develop extraordinary personal relations with clients, and with the companies they deal with. I tend to have very good relationships with management, from the chairman to the president to the chief financial officer of a company. When you have a good relationship, your phone calls are returned first. I have a male colleague who is very confrontational and likes to embarrass management at meetings. Why? It's probably a male ego thing, but it's destructive. Are they going to call him back first, or me? They'll think, I'll phone Mary. I'm not going to call him because he's obnoxious. I think women sometimes have an edge because their egos aren't so much tied up in the game. They know how to exploit the positive side, rather than accentuating the negative."

Mary then commented on a different element of the equation. "I think by and large women are more risk averse. I see this in individual investors, for example, and I think women can naturally be much better investors than men. Men tend to follow the hot tip at the cocktail party; they're seeking the up-and-coming technology stock that's going to double next week. But women tend to be much more thoughtful. It takes them a little longer, but they often make better decisions. They want to understand thoroughly before they act, and they are more often long-term oriented."

Both men and women, however, had to adjust to the computer revolution. As Mary said, "Undeniably, there has been a change in the industry, and I've been forced to change also. In the early '70s, it was definitely a more seat-of-the-pants operation. Decisions were made on gut feelings. Why do you like these stocks? They look cheap, it feels right. Now we've all become quantitatively oriented and dependent on computer models. An analyst has to find the balance; we have very sophisticated tools, but ultimately it's still a judgment call. I've seen analysts make more mistakes because they get so involved with the numbers and the computer model that they lose touch with their own judgment. Those models are only as good as the input, and you can become too dependent on them. I try to reduce risk as much as possible through use of quantitative technique, but ultimately I must make the final call."

Mary leaned forward and raised a finger, as if a new idea had just crossed her mind. "There is another big change today from the '70s. With technology and telecommunications, everything has to happen immediately. In the '70s, you'd get earnings reports from a company, then call the company later that day, look at the numbers, spend another day figuring out what action you should take, and maybe then start calling clients. Now, you're expected to make a judgment call literally as the numbers come over the tape. Our economist waits for the 8:30 A.M. releases, reads the releases as they come out, and then is on an open mike, commenting to all our offices. It's that fast. It's the same thing with analysts. They're expected to be out on the trading floor the moment the earnings come out, saying what this means and what that means. We don't have the luxury of time that we used to. I think it's become a much more demanding profession. It's an extremely high pressure business now."

A seasoned professional (she's weathered a crash and a mini-crash), Mary is more than qualified to advise rookie analysts. She laughed and said, "It takes years and a few market cycles to make solid calls. Young analysts who are doing the morning call will say, 'This is the best company, earnings are going up 20 percent a year. But I rate it neutral because it's selling at its highest P/E in the last decade.' I take them aside and say, 'In a low inflation/low interest rate environment, P/Es get higher. We're justifying a higher P/E on the market because interest rates are so much lower, and we don't think inflation is coming back.' Then I show them the historical P/E ratios and try to explain. But ultimately, being a good analyst is a combination of two factors: being grounded heavily in the quantitative techniques—really looking at the numbers, plus using good judgment gained from many years of experience."

Mary had only positive advice for women wanting to work on Wall Street. "I would say: Just do it," she smiled. "This is a great business. It's extremely interesting and very entrepreneurial. Also, although few people consider this part of it, there is an absolutely terrific feeling when you're right about the market because you help people. We made a great call on bonds in the 1980s, which was to lock in the double digit yields because rates were going down. I have people who come up to me after a seminar and say, 'I just want to thank you. We bought the long-term bonds you recommended and now our monthly income is twice what it would be if we'd stayed in CDs.' You can make a tremendous difference in people's lives."

Ultimately, the most satisfying aspect of Mary's job is knowing her work has a tangible effect on others. She said, "It's really nice to know that you've done a good job and people are going to benefit—and they aren't rich people necessarily. Over 30 percent of people in the United States own mutual funds and they're certainly not all rich. Most of them are people who are saving for college or for retirement. Some are participating in pension funds. I really feel very good when we are right because we're doing a good job for our clients."

As for future plans, Mary concluded, "It's hard to say. When I was in my 20s, I saw very few people in their 40s in this business. It's so grueling and demanding, with such high pressure, that most people don't stay too long beyond their 40s. It's a very hard life, really, and I don't think I could do it for another decade. What I'd like to do next is something involved with investments, while keeping the media exposure. *Wall $treet Week with Louis Rukeyser* has been a tremendous opportunity for me and I've met so many incredible people. When I have dinner with people like John Templeton and Milton Friedman at *Wall $treet Week,* it's pretty exciting. But I would like to do something that gets me out of the constant need to travel."

We walked back through the trading room. CNBC was on all the monitors, which made me smile. I strained to hear, but the racket of shouting traders, ringing phones, and beeping computers drowned out the broadcast. Rock and roll, I thought to myself as I walked past two guys standing no further than a foot apart, each holding two phones and screaming simultaneously at the top of their lungs. I looked back and saw Mary, standing in the midst of all the insanity, hands on her hips, looking right at home.

Bridget Macaskill

President and CEO, Oppenheimer Funds

Negotiating the World Trade Center is no easy trick these days. As a result of the bombing a few years ago, an elaborate web of security measures were put in place. After going through a rigorous series of checks and double checks, I got the all clear, passed through the metal detectors, and headed to the 34th floor and my meeting with Bridget Macaskill.

I wasn't sure what to expect from my interview. I really didn't know much about Bridget other than the fact that she had a terrific reputation on the Street—both as a business woman and a person. She was a bit of an anomaly among the group of women I had assembled for this project: She's a transplant from Britain, where her background was in food marketing; in addition, she entered the

Street through a kind of back door, as a marketing specialist, a less-visible area of the industry. As a result, she provides a fascinating, alternative perspective of the Wall Street experience.

Most people don't think of financial instruments or investments as "products"; they think of investing as a service provided to them by their brokers. But services, just like products, are bought by consumers who demand a certain bang for their buck. As Bridget found when she started working on the Street, true market research and analysis of the needs and wants of the investment "consumer" was virtually nonexistent, at least compared to the work she'd done in the food industry. And ironically, no one was more initially skeptical that such skills would be transferable to the financial arena than Macaskill herself.

Judging by the position (figuratively and literally) she now occupies—President and CEO of Oppenheimer Funds, with a spacious view of the Hudson River from her office—the transition was a success. The most interesting thing about Bridget, though, is her unique take on the Street and her thoughts on success in general. She is a woman with crystal clear priorities, and these lie in the direction of her family—a fact that may surprise those who automatically associate success on Wall Street (especially for women) with sacrifices in the spouse and children areas. "I am not someone who would sacrifice a family for a career. I really wouldn't," she said simply. That she is able to maintain such a stance without compromising her career is a testament to her personal and professional aptitude.

We settled down on a big leather sofa with cups of coffee, and I waited to hear the story of Bridget's ascent. Her background, both socially and professionally, truly did not portend a career on Wall Street. When I asked her if there ever was a time when she envisioned a career like the one she now enjoys, she shook her head decisively.

"People ask me if I set lifetime career goals for myself," she said. "The answer is absolutely not. When I left college, if anyone had sat me down and asked me how long I was going to work, I probably would have said five years. I grew up in a culture that expected women to work until they got married—then they would be housewives. I got into this business totally by accident. Before I arrived on Wall Street, I had been working in the food business in the U.K.—about as far from Wall Street as you can get. I had a typical consumer marketing background. A lot of advertising, a lot of brand strategies."

Bridget worked for one of the largest British corporations, Unigate, straight out of college, and experienced some of the same obstacles familiar to the women who initially broke through the sex barrier on the Street. When she started, they didn't have a single woman in management. Starting out as a "glorified secretary," her inquisitiveness and initiative brought her more responsibilities. After only a year or so, she was put in charge of new products, a role that, while not considered a hot spot within the company, turned out to be a launching pad for her.

She conceived the simple but ingenious notion of delivering fresh orange juice to the door along with the daily milk. Although she was certain the idea would be a hit, it was dismissed by her older, male colleagues. But Bridget was not to be denied. "I said to my boss, 'Listen, I can do this without spending any money. I'll get the carton manufacturers to make the cartons and the juice people to donate the juice,' and I did literally that. I went and talked to the factory manager and I got a little corner of his factory and I borrowed the necessary equipment. Everyone thought I was mad and kind of dismissed it. But it just took off and turned out to be a phenomenal success."

While management was shocked at the project's success, they still did not appear to take the then 24-year-old Bridget seriously. When she subsequently decided she'd have to travel to the United States and Brazil to become an orange juice buyer, the company scoffed, deeming her too young and inexperienced to do the job.

Only when she was able to back them into a corner by announcing she would take her vacation to visit with the juice producers did her bosses grudgingly allow her to take the trip—and then only with a senior male escort.

"My boss's parting words as I went out the door were, 'Well, we expect a report from you. This is not a holiday you are going on,' " Bridget remembered, smiling. "So I came back and I delivered a 150-page report which gave everything—the political and economic backgrounds of the country, how you grow an orange tree and seeds, and grafting and trees and tree culture—every single piece of information they could possibly want."

Such drive led to Bridget's eventual promotion to head of the entire marketing division, in charge of 120 people and overseeing 250 products. But she still had to push to get equal treatment. The day after the promotion, the company's CEO told her, that although her job had always been a main board director's position, they were instituting a new policy: Future directors would serve a probation period before they were put on the board. Bridget was shocked. "I said, 'What? Hold on a minute. When did this policy get introduced?' He said, 'Well, it's new.' I said, 'You're dead right it's new, because this male colleague of mine was made production director six months ago and he didn't serve any probation period.' He said, 'Bridget, this is not my doing, just stick with it.' Basically what happened was the chairman of the company decided he wasn't going to have any 29-year-old on his Board—certainly not any 29-year-old female.

"I was totally incensed," Bridget continued, "and I decided I had two choices: I could either resign, which would achieve nothing and would actually play exactly into his hands so he wouldn't have to deal with this issue, or I could wait six months and then see what he did. The guy who was my direct boss was very supportive. He was as shocked by the whole thing as I was. So, I waited the six months and they *did* put me on the Board. In terms of male chauvinism my experience early on in my career prepared me for everything. By the time I left there were still practically no women in management."

Do you think that was a function of the time or of the type of business that she was in, or is the United Kingdom different than the United States in this regard? I asked. "I think it was a combination of all of those things," Bridget answered. "There are a few more women now, but at the most senior level they still don't really exist in the manufacturing side of food business. Also, in those days British women—even if they had been to university—were expected to get married and have children, and as soon as you started having children you were supposed to stop working. Almost all of my college friends did exactly that."

Bridget has sometimes wondered what course her life might have taken had she remained in England. Whatever might have happened was rendered academic when her husband, to whom she'd been married only a short time, came home from work one day and announced he was being transferred to the States. Despite her own successful career, Bridget decided to give the move a shot. But it was not a smooth transition. She found landing a job in her industry more difficult than she imagined and experienced unexpected difficulties obtaining a visa. Such circumstances made this one of the less enjoyable periods of Bridget's life, one she managed to survive in part because of the strength of her marriage.

"New York is not a city to be in if you have no children, no job and not many friends," she said, shaking her head. "We had a few friends, but you can only meet them for lunch every so often and they go rushing back to work. I did get to visit every museum in the city, but it was a lonely and somewhat difficult time. I didn't get depressed by it, but it was not the easiest period of my life. Thank goodness I was married. I had an anchor and a companion. But my husband was in a new job and he left at 7:00 in the morning and came back at 8:00 or 9:00 at night, which made the day very long."

It wasn't long, however, before Bridget received a fortuitous but unexpected phone call. It did not start out as a potential job opportunity. A headhunter asked Bridget to do a "favor" for them: helping out a client of theirs, a financial services firm recently purchased by a British company who needed someone familiar with marketing in Britain. Bridget initially balked at the idea; she was unfamiliar with finance, and quite honestly, not much interested.

"I told them I couldn't possibly talk to them because I didn't know anything about financial services," she remembered. "They told me I wasn't expected to know about financial services, but to know about marketing in the U.K. If you're looking for a job and a headhunter asks you to do a favor, you just sort of do it. So, I came and talked to the CEO of Oppenheimer who explained to me that he had been asked to set up a mutual fund operation in the U.K.—what could I tell him about marketing in the U.K.?

"I had a really interesting conversation with him. He was sort of intrigued by the whole orange juice story. He said that he wasn't ready to start the business in the U.K., but when he was, perhaps I could do some consulting work for him. I said that would be no problem and I left." Surprisingly, the CEO called Bridget back a few days later and asked her if she'd like to head up marketing for the firm. "I think I laughed," Bridget said, chuckling a little. "I said I didn't think it was a very good idea. Number one, I didn't know anything about marketing in the States, and number two, I didn't know the first thing about financial services. What's more, I didn't even want to work in the financial services industry. He asked me why not, and I said, 'Because it is so boring.' He told me that I clearly didn't understand this business—it was a fabulous business—and wanted me to come down and talk to him again. He basically sold me on the idea on how great the financial services industry was. He was the ultimate salesman."

It may seem somewhat ironic that Bridget virtually had to be force-fed a position that most Wall Street professionals would kill for. Bridget's prospective boss, for one, certainly didn't seem to understand her reluctance.

"He was incensed by my reaction that I didn't want the job, that I didn't even want to be interviewed for the job. He asked me how I could turn down the job when I didn't even have one. Eventually I said to him, 'Look, if you really think I can do this job why don't we say that if I'll come to work with you, you will get me a visa.' To me one of the greatest attractions of this business was that I knew that since they were owned by a British company they could get me a visa like that (she snapped her fingers). So I said, 'I'll come and work here, you get me a visa. By the time my visa arrives if you've decided that you've made a terrible mistake, I will go peacefully and take my visa with me; if I've decided I've made a terrible mistake, you'll let me go and I'll take my visa with me.' " Her future boss agreed, telling her, "You won't regret this for a minute. This will be the greatest career move." Bridget smiled, then added, "He reminds me of this frequently." His words turned out to be prophetic: Bridget immediately found her new field fascinating.

Her concerns about her past work experience being inapplicable in her new environment turned out to be unfounded. In fact, Bridget saw some striking parallels to her 12 years of experience in the U.K. dairy industry, which went from being a one-product, manufacturing-driven business—one kind of milk delivered directly to your door in glass bottles—to being a multiproduct, marketing-driven industry.

Oppenheimer, in a way, was as one-dimensional as the old milk industry, offering primarily aggressive equity funds to its customers. Rather than starting with the needs of customers and developing products for them, Oppenheimer offered investors a very limited product line from which they seemed unwilling to stray. "I think the timing was extraordinarily fortuitous," Bridget noted. "Having lived through a similar situation, I arrived in the mutual fund industry and thought, 'Oh my goodness, I've been here before.'

"At the beginning, I knew nothing about the financial services industry, so I did what I knew how to do, which was to take a market, analyze it, and look at how our products were positioned within it. I found that all our products were skewed toward the aggressive growth end of the market. We 'manufactured' growth funds because it was what we knew how to make, and we believed it was what consumers should invest in, whether they wanted to or not. We knew what was best for them better than they did. As a result, we got into some philosophical discussions about what marketing was. Wall Street in those days, and today in some instances, did not factor the consumer into the equation at all. 'Marketing' really meant 'selling.' If you sold a product and produced a piece of sales literature, it was marketing."

Bridget introduced an element of objective, detailed market research that was previously unknown at Oppenheimer. "This was 1983 and there was absolutely no concept of starting with the consumers and discovering what the consumer needed and designing a product to meet their needs. We would produce these television commercials advertising a fund, but nobody measured the responses—nobody knew whether these ads were successful or not. I think one of the reasons I was hired was that the CEO believed that I would kind of run the advertising side of the business. What I ultimately persuaded him to do was to stop advertising completely because we were advertising products that weren't on the shelf: We didn't have enough distribution of our funds to justify advertising." Bridget was silent for a moment. "It took a lot of years to win that battle," she concluded.

In the course of doing her job, Bridget found herself coming into contact with other areas of the company that were not used to interacting. "I came into this organization and started trying to do some different things and I found that I needed to work with the portfolio group, which in those days was in a separate half of the floor. There was a door that divided them from the rest of the organization. If you went through the door and went to talk to some of them they would say, 'Oh, you must be lost, you shouldn't be down here.' I would say, 'I came to talk to you about the fact that I am going to run an advertising campaign on your fund. What are you going to do if you get a lot more money to manage? Is that going to be a problem?' They would respond, 'You don't talk to us about advertising, you talk to the CEO about advertising.' I said, 'But this is your fund. Aren't you interested in what we are going to say about it, what the repercussions might be?' "

Bridget's desire to bridge the gap between the investment, back-office sales, and marketing sides of the business was considered unnecessary at the time and ruffled a few feathers among those who saw no reason to upset the status quo. "I was constantly calling people up in other areas of the business and saying we're planning to do this, can you do that? And they would call my boss and say, 'What is Bridget doing? She keeps phoning us with all these issues. Nobody bothered us with all these problems before.' "

While she was confronting these challenges in the workplace, Bridget also had developments on the home front that allowed her to experience another side of her adopted industry. "By the time I got my visa I was also pregnant," she explained. "It was not good timing. I remember vividly going to this man who had hired me and telling him I'm very sorry, but I need to take some vacation. He asked me how much and I said about three months. He said, 'This is not the U.K., this is America. You don't get three months vacation.' I said, 'You don't quite understand, I'm pregnant.'

The next day her boss called her into his office and told Bridget to go to England the following week to get a nanny so she could be back at work within three weeks after having the baby. "I told him I didn't want to come back after three weeks. I came from a background where, when you had a first child, you didn't go back to work, and I had a boss who assumed I would come back three weeks later. I remember thinking, 'What do I do about this?' I decided maybe I should just stay until after the baby was born and see how I felt."

In retrospect, Bridget feels that in the early months, her attitude towards her job helped her not to feel frustrated. "In that first year, I wasn't sure how long I would stay in that job. Maybe that influenced whether I was more or less frustrated. Maybe it was also because of the obstacles I had experienced back in the Unigate days where people would say to the me, 'No you can't do this and no you can't do that.' I always naively assumed that they had good business reasons, but it took me a long time to latch onto the fact that they didn't like cooperating with some 25-year-old woman. I was so used to that happening that it didn't even bother me anymore and I did not let it stand in my way. Probably one of the things that has been a real benefit to me in whatever job I've done has been the fact that when people said no to me I never assumed it was because I was a woman. It took me a long time to realize that *was* actually the real reason. My first reaction wasn't, 'Oh they're doing that because I'm a woman,' it was, 'Oh well they're obviously too busy or they don't think this is a good idea or I haven't expressed myself properly or I haven't explained the problem. I'll just try it another way,' and I never got terribly hung up about chauvinism. I just sort of went on."

Bridget echoed the sentiment I'd heard expressed a number of different ways by a number of different women: You just have to push it aside, you just go forward. "You really don't focus on it," she continued. "At Unigate it wasn't until somebody threw it straight in my face and said, 'You are not going to be put on the Board' that I stopped and said, 'I don't believe this.' Then the reason for it was absolutely inescapable, but I decided I wasn't going to let it get the better of me."

Bridget's specialty in marketing raised eyebrows in general on the Street. "People would say to me, 'What are you doing on Wall Street? You've got a marketing job? What's a marketing job?' It just wasn't done. The combination of being female, being British, and having a marketing job was a little unusual, to say the least. I do remember one man saying to me, 'You shouldn't be here. You should be at home. Why aren't you at home looking after your children?' I said to him, 'Do you have any daughters?' and he said, 'Yes, and they're just as bad as you. They're working too.' "

I mentioned to Bridget that when I first started in broadcasting my specialty was the futures markets. I had to call the pits in Chicago, and they were very surprised to hear a woman's voice. But in a way, it kind of worked for me; after they got over the initial shock, I could try to use it to my advantage.

Bridget's experience was a little different. "I don't think that was true for me at the beginning," she said. "People were either neutral or negative about it. I would say in the last five years it has become a benefit because it's unusual to find a woman in a senior position. I have no doubt that I get to do some things, or get interviewed on a particular subject, because I am a female. It's a mixed blessing. I sometimes wish I could be identified as a CEO of a major firm, not always as a 'female' CEO."

Interestingly, Bridget found herself having to make the effort to make some of her male colleagues more comfortable with the idea of working with a woman—not the other way around. "I think in some cases the men who had worked all of their lives in a very male environment found it very uncomfortable to suddenly have a woman there," she said. "In the U.K., for example, this was a chummy group of men who went off to their Board meetings, had dinner in the evening, drinking what they liked and telling the jokes they liked, and they didn't want to change their behavior because of some *girl*. In the U.S. the dynamic is different, but there are still some men on Wall Street who have been there all their lives, who have never had to interact with women in a business context. They find it very restrictive. *They* find it awful not to be able to tell their jokes and make sexist remarks—things that are sort of second nature to them. They don't quite know how to react around women, whether to hold the door open or not. It became an absolute standing joke in this company that everybody would always say to me at any meeting, 'Bridget, where is the coffee?' and what I chose to do about that was to make it very clear—in a good-humored way—that I was not there to get the coffee. But normally I got the coffee anyway."

She paused for a moment when she noticed my surprise at this comment. I asked her how she could do that. "You just make a big joke out of it." she explained. "Sometimes I would make them go get the coffee and most of them didn't know how to make it. One of the things that I also believe is that it doesn't really help to show up and embarrass men who find it difficult to interact with women, because all it does is compound the problem. If you make a big deal out of the fact that they made a remark that they certainly shouldn't have made—when in most cases they are not really aware of having said it—you escalate the whole issue and increase the level of discomfort. Fortunately, we are now at the stage where there are enough women in senior positions throughout the company that we challenge such remarks by saying, 'What did you just say?' But you do it in a funny kind of way, with a sense of humor. You say, 'Hey, you need to go to feminist training school.' "

I noted that it's much the same in the newsroom. You can get so much more accomplished with a funny barb than you can with a sensitivity seminar. "Exactly," Bridget responded. "There is no doubt that once in a while in any organization, there can be real problems. Women may feel threatened or harassed. You deal with these situations and you deal with them very seriously and very quickly. In some cases these men simply don't realize that they are being offensive. There have been times when I have taken somebody aside after an incident and said, 'Do you have any idea what you just did?' They look at me and say, 'What did I just do? Did I say something wrong?' They really don't know."

Bridget seems unusually good-natured (or, maybe more accurately, thick-skinned), and I wanted to get her feelings on another issue I had talked to other women about: They think Wall Street is essentially gender neutral because it's a bottom-line business—if you perform, you get the money. Would you agree, I asked, or is that really a separate issue?

"I think it's a separate issue," Bridget said. "It's one of the big issues on Wall Street, and it has to do with why you see more women in senior positions in certain parts of Wall Street. But Wall Street is not totally uniform. I think there are some cultures in which women have a natural management style."

When I pointed out that there are differences between men and women's management styles, Bridget elaborated. "I think that women naturally are good motivators, good at juggling different projects and issues at the same time, and more cooperative rather than aggressive and confrontational. There are certain parts of Wall Street where that management style works better. In typical brokerage houses, in trading situations, there is more aggression. Certainly, in the '80s it was much more aggressive, competitive, a lot of egos involved, and I think many women opted out because they simply didn't want to work in that culture. It didn't have anything to do with ability, or whether they could hack it or not, it had to do with the fact that at the end of the day they decided that wasn't where they wanted to work. We have a lot of women here who came from brokerage firms and what you tend to hear from them is, "This environment is such a relief. We don't have to constantly look over our shoulders and watch our backs, be political, aggressive, and pushy."

A common refrain among Wall Street women is the admission of having "no life," at least in terms of what most people would consider "normal" work hours or adequate family time. The pace and the pressure sometimes rule that out. Bridget asserted that women *don't* have to live that way. Contrary to stereotypes, she sees plenty of opportunity for women who don't necessarily want to look up and see the office clock strike midnight when they've been at work since 7:00 A.M.

"On Wall Street there are some jobs that I think are wonderful jobs for women who want to have a life outside of their work," she said. "If you are working in a business that is dictated by market hours and you can be here by 8:30 in the morning and out by 6:00 P.M., you can actually be at home in the evenings and see your kids and your spouse and have a life. I do know this is one of the reasons I am still working. Sure, I work plenty of nights, I travel a lot, but it's controllable. It is unusual for me to be told at 6:00 P.M. that I have to be here until midnight. I would not do it if that was what it took. I want a life outside work. When I talk to some of my female friends who have given up, they tend to be lawyers, investment bankers, in advertising, in businesses where you are really at the beck and call of a client—and if the client needs you at midnight, you are there at midnight. I think that is one of the reasons why you don't get many women in professions like investment banking and even in high-powered corporate law offices. There aren't too many women who want to do that."

It's somewhat refreshing to hear another woman, especially such a well-respected, successful one, voice the opinion that you don't have to do it all. I think women still feel they are put in the position of deciding whether they want home and family or a career—one or the other. It's somewhat unforgiving. I told Bridget some of the women I work with who have children still assume the majority of the responsibility for the family.

Bridget agreed, and conceded that her particular work situation is probably more forgiving than most. Her attitude is also reflected in her management style. "Absolutely. This is a very flexible organization. If you want to go to your child's school play, you should go to the school play. If people work hard, work long hours and do a great job, and then take two hours off in the morning, why should I care? I don't even want to know." She still sees a difference between the attitudes of men and women, though. "I still hear 'I won't do that' from the men. Many men still believe that it's okay for women to adjust their schedules to meet family demands, but not men—they seem to think there are different rules for men and women. I encourage men to take time for their families also, I believe it would actually help the family situation because it would provide some relief to their wives, but they mostly don't do it. Sometimes if a man works long hours and several weekends in a row, I say to him 'Why don't you just take Monday off. Go home, be with your family. I don't want his wife saying, "I hate that company, I hate that job because I never see my husband. I think if people find balance in their lives they are happier people, they are more productive people."

I am surprised, and a little disappointed, I told Bridget, that this hasn't changed because it's more essential now for women to be part of the breadwinning pair; it's somewhat expected that if you go to college, you don't necessarily get married and have kids—you have a career. I asked Bridget if she thought being a female manager made her more sensitive to these considerations. She nodded, "I think it does. I think that now that there are enough women here that such flexibility is built into the culture, people do feel more comfortable. Now more men will say to me, 'I want to take some time because my daughter has a game,' or whatever.

As far as dealing with stress, Bridget exhibits a degree of practicality. "I don't feel sorry for myself that I don't have 'time for me,' she said simply. "I don't expect to have time to get to do many of the things that I would like to do. That is something that I do not have. But I am also very conscious of the fact that I could stop work and have all the time in the world, so I better not complain about not having time for me."

As befits someone who preaches the value of finding a balance between the personal and professional aspects of life, Bridget is sure to make time for her children. "I have two boys," she said. "When I go home at night I am totally happy in the evening doing their homework with them, playing with them, reading to them. I can walk into the house and go straight into the French test the next day or the project that our nine-year-old has to do. I can sit down and do whatever or play with them."

Bridget admitted that it's not easy, and that she, of course, is not perfect—it's simply her priority in the evening. "I really try to be home by 7:00 P.M. to spend the time until they go to bed with them. That immediately switches me off from work and switches me into their lives. At some point at 8:00 or 9:00 I'll sit and have a drink with my husband and talk about what happened during the day; but I don't go and exercise for an hour, I don't go and lie in a bathtub and soak. I guess that's the choice you make." When I told Bridget it sounds like she thrives on adversity, she responded that it's as if her energy level is proportional to the challenges and duties she faces. "I do think that having a high energy level and having the ability to juggle has really helped," she said, adding, "I have a very clear sense of priorities. If my family needs me they come first."

Bridget admitted to being torn at times, but family is worth it to her; the secret is standing firm. "Once in a while, I will be in a meeting at 6:00 P.M. when I have promised that I will do something with one of my children or my husband, and I have stood up and said, 'I'm very sorry, but I am going to leave this meeting now,' and I've always told them why. I don't do it all the time—if I did it every other day I think people would get very tired of it. But as it is, people have sort of accepted it, I think that because I am sort of unequivocal and up-front about it. You have to organize your life, though—you can't do it every day. But there are times when your family needs to be shown they're more important than the job."

Bridget's coworkers and colleagues are nearly unanimous in their praise for her, a point she found embarrassing when I mentioned it to her. They said she seemed to have an intuition about people and that she's devoted to what she does. She both encourages intimacy and commands respect. She recounted a story that revealed her feelings about her work.

"The day I was named CEO, we called a meeting of senior managers. I hadn't prepared a speech. I just had some ideas I wanted to share with the organization. So I stood up there and started saying how proud I was of this company, and how much I cared about this place, and how impressed I was by the people who work here. It was highly personal, very emotional, and, suffice to say, not the "vision thing" you might expect from a CEO on her first day. So I stopped and said, "Oh, my God. Here I am meant to be your fearless leader and I can't even take command of my own presentation.

"But," Bridget continued, "it affected me because I *do* care desperately about this organization, about the people who work here. I care about them in a very—and this is not always good—in a very personal way. When people here have problems they get huge support. If anybody here is sick or if anybody has real family problems, this organization really extends itself, provided that they are employees who have given to the company, who have been loyal, who've worked hard."

While Bridget is well liked and respected, she admitted she's also very demanding. "I expect people to work hard. This is an organization that sets very high standards, but doesn't mean you can never make a mistake. We have a Statement of Shared Values, which we expect people to live. It talks about excellence, integrity, caring, and team spirit—things I believe in firmly. It's like a two-way street. If we expect people to give a lot to this company, we owe them a lot in return. But that's why I don't care if they go to the school play, or go and see their father in the hospital, or whatever they have to do. I am really intolerant of people that don't try hard enough, who kind of coast."

Besides her clear sense of priorities and high energy level, Bridget had to think for a moment about specific reasons for her success. "I do have very high standards for myself—I expect a lot of myself. I am not a perfectionist in the sense of wanting *everything* to be perfect." She gestured toward her desk, a mess of piled papers and reports. "I mean look at this," she laughed. "But I won't settle for second best from me. I wish I was less demanding with other people, especially those that are close to me.

"My husband says to me sometimes about our kids, 'Bridget, they're children. They are not perfect and they are not going to be perfect. Don't expect too much of them. You can't impose your standards on them.' He's right and it's wonderful he's there to say it to me. He sometimes stops me when I'm saying to them, 'Have you really done this homework project as well as you could possibly do it?' They are very active, normal, energetic boys without a very intense sense of the importance of homework. I tend to be the one who says, 'Don't you think we ought to go over the French for tomorrow's test once more?' and my husband says to me, 'Leave it alone, that's enough.' "

But for herself, she remains demanding and persistent. "I don't give up very easily," she added. "If I run into an obstacle or a barrier, I get focused on the end goal. If I have to maneuver my way around something, I'll find a way to maneuver my way around it." She considered for a moment. "I think the ability to build relationships probably helps, too."

While her uncompromising commitment to her family may seem like a dragging weight in the professional world, Bridget sees it as one of her greatest strengths. "It has allowed me to make braver decisions," she noted. "I think sometimes having the courage to make it very clear to everybody that I know there is life outside work helps. I still think it is very tough for women to juggle. It's very sad that so many women get to the top of their profession making sacrifices along the way. I don't know how to even start resolving that issue."

Bridget stared out the window, lost in thought. "I look around me and I do not see many women who have reached the most senior levels with their husbands and children and outside lives intact. I would never pretend that it is easy—it isn't. There are days when it's really tough, but as long as it goes fine most days, it's worth it. Who knows? I hope my children will turn out okay, because if they don't I will feel guilty. It's an issue women deal with all of the time—it's probably the hardest thing to come to terms with.

"You have to keep a sense of perspective," Bridget stressed. "Any one organization can survive without one individual, but families can't. Families need parents."

Spoken by someone who knows.

Mei Ping Yang

Vice President and Proprietary Trader, Goldman Sachs

For most people, especially those outside New York, Greenwich Village brings to mind images of aspiring writers, musicians, and actors hanging out in local bars and cafes, living in sparsely furnished apartments, struggling to make ends meet. For nearly all this century, the Village has been the de facto center of bohemian life in New York, if not the country. While the area has become more gentrified in recent years (much to the disgruntlement of many longtime locals), it still retains an almost European charm and individuality. Beautiful old brown- and grey-stone apartment buildings and town homes line the curving, tree-lined streets, peppered here and there with small shops, clubs, and restaurants.

It was not the neighborhood I would have expected a trader to pick as a rendezvous for a talk about life in the markets. Downtown, close to the Street, or even midtown would have seemed more likely. But this is where Mei Ping Yang, a proprietary trader for Goldman Sachs, wanted to meet. I happily agreed.

By her own estimation, Mei Ping has handled up to a half billion dollars at any given time in the international currency markets. That's *billion*. One would expect such a player to be a loud, aggressive, outgoing character, all brag and boast (and most likely a man). Mei Ping is no such person. She has managed to find her niche in the trading world and has effected a wonderful mesh between it and her seemingly untraderlike personality. She's quiet, reserved—her responses to questions are deliberate and thoughtful. Given that she describes herself as "pathologically shy," I was all the more surprised by her desire to hold the interview at a crowded restaurant down in the Village—outside on the brick patio, packed so tight the wait staff had trouble maneuvering between the tables. On a warm, inviting spring day like the one on which we met, the Village is crowded, pulsing, and noisy: Street vendors and small shopkeepers hawk their wares on the curb, tourists wander slowly down the streets, locals crisscross quickly between them on their way to favorite local haunts, rollerbladers and cyclists cut through the crowds, almost oblivious to their surroundings, and music blares from a thousand storefronts and open apartment windows. It didn't seem like the preferred hangout of a "retiring" personality. Speaking in a low, quiet voice (with a slight Asian accent) that was sometimes difficult to hear above the din, Mei Ping nevertheless seemed to enjoy the somewhat chaotic surroundings. Perhaps as a trader it is second nature to her to be calm and composed in a hectic environment—and privately enjoy the spectacle that surrounds her.

Mei Ping is truly an international woman: Born in Singapore, she also lived in Malaysia for 10 years. Her father is a merchant and her mother an artist. Prior to her present position with Goldman, Sachs &

Company, she served as a portfolio manager in international investment advisory with Bankers Trust, where she was responsible for discretionary foreign exchange overlay for $1.3 billion in high net-worth portfolios and $400 million in institutional global fixed income portfolios. She also worked in foreign exchange sales in the international private banking division of Bankers Trust in Singapore. She traces much of her success to her upbringing, and maintains something of the aura of the child from humble beginnings who has made good.

Mei Ping is a relatively new transplant to New York—to the United States, for that matter (although she lived in the U.S. from 1980–1986). Until a few years ago, she plied her trade in Singapore, which, with the presence of the Singapore International Monetary Exchange (SIMEX), has emerged as a key center of the powerful Pacific Rim economy. It was there that she originally learned the ropes of currency trading.

Although Mei Ping was a finance major, she was not necessarily intent on entering the markets from a young age. Her academic background included a lot of history courses, and she was initially drawn to trading because of its global aspects—but she really knew nothing about trading, per se, and approached her future career somewhat naively. "I always knew I wanted to be involved in something 'international,' but I didn't really know exactly what I wanted to be," she recalled. "When I was in graduate school, I took a class called International Finance and Trade, and I thought to myself, 'I think I'll do currency trading.' " Noting my surprise that someone would just decide to "do currency trading," Mei Ping smiled and continued. "Well, yeah. It's kind of funny, but I wanted something very involved that would take up all of my time, and literally combine every aspect of my life."

Trading certainly fits that bill, but I found it interesting that Mei Ping was initially drawn to these intellectual facets of the business rather than just the money. She expressed a degree of surprise at how outsiders view the business she's in. "Trading has such an aura of, I guess, glamour, about it. When people ask me, especially young people, what's involved in trading, it's odd . . ." she trailed off for a moment, thinking it over. "I think people get too caught up in the glamour and the money. You can almost see a little shine in their eyes when they think of all the money we handle."

Mei Ping's focus is elsewhere, and her relationship to the market is more than a little philosophical. "When I'm asked why I trade, or what enables me to trade the way I do, I guess I give a rather atypical answer. I basically say the real ingredient you must have is self-knowledge, because what you will find, and what I found in trading, was a journey to find myself, to know myself."

In the trading game, those unfortunate souls who do not "know themselves," who do not understand the pressures of the game and how they'll perform under the type of stress only the markets provide, may soon find themselves losing their profits or their jobs. While Mei Ping seems to navigate the straits of the markets with as much calm and objectivity as anybody I've spoken to, she is not oblivious to how trading can skew your perspective; it is precisely because she understands this part of the business that she can cope with it. "What happens in trading is that time seems to become compressed," she said, "and your buttons are pushed faster. It becomes sensory overload to a certain degree—only trading can do that to you."

In retrospect, Mei Ping was lucky that she got the opportunity to test out her independence and trading skills early on in her career. "I started working in Singapore for a small Norwegian bank," she said. "Actually, it was only small in Singapore, but it was a very large bank in Norway. I ended up working with an incredible man— someone I don't think you could find in this business anymore— who, after my having worked just a week or so in trading, said, 'Here, you can do this, trade under my limit'—indicating his trading umbrella. It could have been very devastating, because if I'd really bombed out, it could have created a lot of problems. I never really had a mentor in that situation, it was just, 'Here, go ahead, do it, kid.' "

As she recounted this rather amazing episode of her story, Mei Ping continued to speak in the same quiet tone, betraying little of what her feelings may have been at the time. Some of the women I've talked to, I told Mei Ping, say they got to where they are because they started very young and were too naive to know that they *should* have been worried or scared. "Exactly," she responded. But when I asked her, she admitted to having been somewhat intimidated. "In a way I was, but when you're young and you have nothing to lose, that fear is very minimal," she explained.

Her timing couldn't have been better. Singapore was coming out of an economically depressed period and was taking the first steps that would eventually transform it into the Asian financial hub it is today. Possibilities seemed limitless, and Mei Ping was as caught up as anybody in what she describes as the infectious, "can-do" spirit of the times. Her initial foray into trading, she remembers, was a successful one.

"It was really interesting," she said, smiling, "I actually made money!" However, she quickly added, "But there was a period where every bloody trade I made was wrong. Those are the dark times, when you just say, 'Jeez, what's the story?' But what I find interesting is when you look at the history of people who go into trading—at least in my experience—normally in the first year, you have an attrition rate of 70 percent and in the second year another 70 percent—maybe not leaving the industry, but leaving trading."

She pondered the reasons for this and described a little of the journey to "self-knowledge" that can accompany a trading career. "I think you begin to realize that you really can't trade, or perhaps you've just been lucky and have managed to escape the hatchet for a while. By the third year you really begin to question whether you can really do this or not, and by the fifth year you either say, 'Hey, I don't want to deal with this anymore' and you get out, or you decide to stay on for the long haul. But by the seventh year you think, 'Well, I think I can make money in this,' and then you come full circle again."

Mei Ping has been a currency trader for 10 years now, so she has had the opportunity to experience this cycle at least once through and has obviously avoided disaster. I asked her if she still enjoys it. "Oh yes. You do have your ups and downs, and there are times when you wonder, 'How come every trade I do seems to be going wrong?' But then you have to remember that's part of the statistics of trading as well, and that you will eventually hit a winning patch. Also, I find it really interesting that you develop an incredible resiliency. There are times when there does not seem to be any humor left, you know, and everything becomes *too* serious. When that happens you just have to say to yourself, 'All right, you've done this before, you've gone through periods when you've made no money—you've lost money from January through October and you've made it all back.' It amounts to recognizing that pattern you've gone through before. You have to be an eternal optimist, but at the same time balance it with a reality check."

A wise philosophy, but one I thought might be difficult to maintain with so much money on the line. I had heard that Mei Ping had traded in very large figures, but I was curious to find out exactly how big. "Well . . . it depends," she said, somewhat reluctantly. "In the beginning, I juggled $5 million. At a certain point, it was all the way up to $500 to $600 million. But I think one of the ways I've always coped with that aspect of it is to never think of the money in absolute terms. I always turn it into percentage terms; you don't think of amounts—that's irrelevant. One day earlier in my career when I was at Bankers Trust someone forced me to sit down and figure out the total amounts I had outstanding in my trades, and when I did, I said, 'What?' It was hard to believe."

The currency market is the largest sector of the international financial marketplace. The activities of governments, central banks, investment banks, global corporations, and huge speculators converge on this segment of the global economy. Mei Ping has traded across the currency spectrum over the course of her career. "Theoretically, I've traded all of them," she noted. "At the moment I'm a bit of a stick in the mud because I'm just trading the major currencies and cross-rates, but that has not been what I've traditionally done. There were periods in my life, especially when I was at Bankers Trust in Singapore, when I put on trades that were Swedish versus Malaysian, whatever took my fancy."

It seems like such a daunting proposition. What are the main tools you use in analyzing these markets? I asked. "Well, I've always had technical analysis—I discovered it about a month after I joined the Norwegian bank. I basically started charting and found it made sense. Also, I watched the spot traders and wondered how they knew when to buy and sell—it was very confusing to me—so I thought there must be some methodology, something that's much more conventional and logical. Also, my boss was charting. He put me in front of my first Teletrac screen [one of the original charting and technical analysis computer programs], and that was the end of me and fundamentals forever."

I was curious to know more about her status as a female trader in Singapore. Westerners often have the impression of many Asian societies, like Singapore, as being extremely strict and very male-dominated. I wasn't sure if these ideas held true, but I did want to know if Mei Ping experienced any discrimination when she started out in Singapore. "I think in spot currencies there are some biases," she said, shrugging a little, "but what surprised Linda Raschke when she came to Singapore was that about 50 percent of the attendees at a trading conference we were at were women. At a similar seminar in the U.S. you'd be lucky if 10 percent were women. But again, Singapore is a very unusual country. Recently, one of our people was visiting the central bank in Singapore and there were 15 traders there. Only five were men, the rest were women. In fact, our de facto central banker has always been a woman. I think it's because Singapore has always had something of a meritocracy." As a result, Mei Ping is not inclined to see much discrimination in the business. "It's obvious that money talks," she said. "You know, how much you make for the company is what really matters."

With things going so well in Singapore, I wondered why Mei Ping would leave, as she eventually did. I found out it was that bane of modern corporate life—the transfer—that resulted in her move to the States. Her work had made her a known quantity on the other side of the ocean. "I was working in the private banking arm of Bankers Trust in the sales and advisory areas. I not only disseminated information for people in Singapore, but also for people in Asia and for product managers in Switzerland and New York, so people were aware of what I did. They wanted somebody to do the currency management for the private clients, so they asked me to join them in New York, and I came over in November of 1992." Despite her strong and longtime ties to Singapore, Mei Ping enjoys her adopted city. "I've *always* liked New York—I'm a city slicker," she joked. "I miss Singapore, though—my family is still there—but so far, every year either I've gone home or my parents have come over here to visit, and every Sunday I call home to let them know I'm all right in this big city. After all, it is halfway around the world—literally."

Because the currency market is truly global, trading around the clock in one financial center or another, Mei Ping is never very far from her work. "I get into the office around 7:30 A.M. and attend meetings, et cetera. But what's really important is that I have two periods of concentrated thinking, in the morning and in the evening. Depending on how things are, if the markets are clear enough, the research I've done in the evening will carry over into the morning. So I plan my moves, I put on trades and see them executed, and hopefully they work out. The rest of the day is spent following the markets, seeing whether they're doing what we think they're supposed to do—hopefully they are—and we test new ideas. I like to do that—test against other traders."

Because she is so soft-spoken, I felt compelled to ask her how she copes with the competitive nature of Wall Street. "I think it's just a matter of keeping yourself sharp, because the market is always changing. There are times when certain models you've constructed work very well, and then suddenly you notice every trade you put on with this particular model is a dud, and you think, 'Oh no, there's something wrong with this.' But you can't *wait* for it to become a dud. When something's working, you've got to continually search out and test other ideas in the market, continue to read. I used to spend a lot of my own money buying software—trading software— just to see different ways of thinking. If I can understand why someone else is thinking in a particular way, then I can apply it to what I do. If the idea doesn't fit, I can put it to rest. But I have yet to find something that I have not learned from. Even though it's just one item, it's an item that adds on to another, and another, and another."

You seem very analytical, very logical, I noted. Given the rational and methodical way she approaches the markets, I had expected Mei Ping to be heavily steeped in traditional economics, mathematics, and maybe computer science. Nothing could have been further from the truth.

"I studied a lot of history," she said. "To use an oft-repeated phrase—history repeats itself. I don't know if this is logical, but I tend to see broad-based patterns in the market that way. There's also a lot of cyclical history in the markets, and that has always been my area of interest—to see the 'repeatability.' One book I enjoyed immensely is *Chaos* by James Lee. When I read that book, I think, 'This is exactly what I want to convey to people.' For example, things repeat, but not in exactly the same fashion. You won't get something that repeats down to the last iota, but you get the general pattern, and as long as you can latch on to that, you have it.

"Don't get me wrong," Mei Ping continued, raising her voice a little, perhaps feeling like she made trading sound too easy, "I always see the markets as a challenge. For example, some people say, 'I beat the market.' I would *never* say that. I would say rather, 'I worked *with* the market,' because let me tell you something, you never really beat a market, and if you try to beat a market, it will beat the shit out of *you*. I have always considered the market to be bigger than I am, so philosophically speaking, the only way in which I think I can make money is to understand what the market is trying to tell me, and then get on to the bandwagon."

Her novel, understated approach to the markets carries over to her self-image. As she mentioned earlier, Mei Ping believes in the importance of knowing yourself. Many traders form inflated opinions of themselves when they're on hot streaks; others seem to develop exaggerated egos as a kind of defense mechanism against the psychological punishment the markets routinely dispense. Mei Ping has no such problem. She doesn't want to fight the market and she doesn't believe she's the savior of her profession.

"Oh, I don't think you should have an ego at all," she said. "The people I have observed who have been in this business for a while—certainly longer than I have—have egos in that they are very centered, they know what they are. But in terms of being 'egotistical,' I would say they are not. They'll always be the first to tell you, the day you think you are a big shot is the day the market will humble you so fast and so hard—" she broke off, shaking her head, "so I don't really think there are egos, especially in markets where you have no control. If you are a very big fish in a very small pond, then, yes, you can have a big ego, because you can control everything.

"But one of the things I learned when I was working for the bank in Singapore was that I was dealing with a lot of wealthy people—some of them were trading—and I found out that sometimes they have built up these conglomerates, these huge businesses, and they are so used to power, so used to saying, 'Jump!' and people saying, 'How high?' that they even try to say that to the market: 'I think you should be going here, and I expect you to be going there.' But as far as the market is concerned, they have no idea what they're talking about, especially the currency market—it's *so* huge. Maybe in the stock market you can get away with that, especially a very small sector, but in the currency market, it's like taking a tea cup and dipping it into the ocean and saying, 'The tide should not be coming up, let me take a teacup and push it back.' " Mei Ping threw up her hands. "It's impossible! The best analogy I can give you is that it's like being a boat on the ocean. Sometimes it seems so huge that you see no land, and you think, 'Gee, I'm so bloody vulnerable.' So when you see a squall coming, the smart thing to do is to take cover—the last thing you want to do is fight it."

Similar to the truce she has declared with the markets, so too has Mei Ping reconciled herself to the compromises she must make in her personal life because of her chosen career. To hear her tell it, though, it seems like a manageable situation. "Because of the 24-hour-a-day aspect of the market," she said, "you constantly have to think about what might happen while you sleep—unlike the U.S. stock market where you can go to bed and then think about tomorrow, unless, of course, there's some huge incident that occurs. But again, you develop coping mechanisms, you carry a beeper that keeps you updated, and when you're with friends, they know you're still listening to them even though you're looking at your beeper all the time. You just learn to live with it; you plan more dinners for Fridays and Saturdays when you want to impress people, or for dates, and then you can be more playful. Yes, there are times when you hate the damn thing because everything you do is wrong. But when you get things right, you realize one of the reasons you really like this is because you've managed to hit all the right spots—and that gives great satisfaction."

When I asked Mei Ping about the people who have had a strong influence on her life and career, she points immediately to another woman: her mother, a bedrock of support and common sense. "When I first started trading," she remembered, "I was very miserable and worried, and she just said, 'You can either be miserable, child, or you can figure out how to change that.' This was when I was losing money trading, and I was very unhappy. But my mom always looked forward. 'The past is the past,' she'd tell me, 'Always be bigger than your misfortunes.'

She learned such lessons well over the years; and, true to her belief in self-knowledge, she came to realize that she has the ultimate control over the stress of her profession. "In terms of coping, I think pressures in the market are mostly internal—ask any trader. People are always surprised when I tell them I'm a trader because they think I should be hyper, speak faster, yell a lot. I think proprietary traders as a whole are very soft-spoken: If you were to make a film about us, it would be the most boring thing in the world. We read, we think—it's very different from spot trading. In proprietary trading, you hardly hear a scream. I also think one of the biggest mistakes people make is to impose their own belief systems on the market. I'd be lying to you if I said I don't look at the market in a particular way—we all have our blind spots."

But you seem to have a very nonadversarial relationship with the market, I noted, almost a friendship. "A friend . . . yes, or perhaps a very bad spouse on occasion," she laughed. "But we all get scared trading the market. The key is to stay with your plan—always stay with your plan. I have a very simple goal, actually: to be a better trader. It's the only thing I know, and it's a form of professional pride. It's what I do."

Daylight was fading, and Mei Ping had to be at work early the next day. The crowd at the restaurant was thinning out: a lull until the late-night business. We said our good-byes and I waved as Mei Ping's cab pulled away. I checked my watch and was surprised to see that over three hours had passed. Our waiter must have been a little exasperated. But at least, in honor of Mei Ping, I had decided to forego my credit card and pay the bill . . . with currency.

Elizabeth Bramwell

Bramwell Capital Management

A Fifth Avenue address is hardly the place you'd expect to find one of Wall Street's busiest money managers. Historically, they have set up shop close to the New York Stock Exchange in lower Manhattan. After double-checking the address I had written down, I left the hum of business activity on the Street and took the long train ride uptown, where, after I got off the train, I found myself amid a mass of holiday shoppers crowding from one store to the next. A short (but challenging) walk brought me to a typical upper-east-side 30-story office building that Bramwell Capital Management calls home. It is here that Elizabeth Bramwell manages some $400 million in assets for mutual funds, endowments, and select public and private pension funds.

Liz's office is a stark contrast to the glitz of Fifth Avenue below, especially during the holidays when everything in New York is adorned with greenery, bows, and sparkling lights. Surprisingly austere, lacking even a single chair in the reception area, Bramwell Capital Management headquarters are small and simple. In complete contrast to most firms in this business, everyone has his or her own office—no cubicles, no large and noisy trading room. No yelling, no screaming. The atmosphere is quiet and studious, reminiscent of a library or law firm. One could easily concentrate in this setting, and that is obviously Liz's intention. Indeed, when you walk into Bramwell Capital Management, you immediately think, *it's all business here.*

But the reality is that Liz and her staff of six have hardly had time to settle into their new surroundings, let alone think about the accoutrements of the office. Since founding the firm in February 1994 after splitting with Mario Gabelli, Bramwell has been working nonstop on her own investment management company, focusing on growth equities. In August 1994, she started The Bramwell Growth Fund, a no-load diversified mutual fund with over $100 million under management as of year-end 1995. A Fifth Avenue address is the logical choice for her, she says. Liz and her staff attend hundreds of analyst meetings and conferences each year, most of which are held either at the nearby swank Plaza Hotel or the equally elegant St. Regis and Pierre Hotels. Besides, with today's communications technology, she doesn't need to be on the Street anymore.

Prior to founding her own company, Liz spent eight years with Gabelli Funds, starting as director of research. She created the investment policy for The Gabelli Growth Fund and, when it launched in April 1987, became its president, chief investment officer, and a trustee. Under her management, the fund appreciated almost 200 percent and amassed assets that, at the time of her departure, were valued at some $700 million. She left the firm in early 1994 over disputes concerning support staff and the abrupt relocation of her New

York office and files to Gabelli's headquarters in suburban Rye. Subsequent to her departure, a dispute over compensation resulted in a favorable NASD (National Association of Securities Dealers) arbitration award of approximately one million dollars to Bramwell.

Standing at her office window, we had a perfect view of Central Park's Wollman Ice Rink and the west side where she grew up. In the distance is the Museum of Natural History, a frequent haunt for Liz as a child growing up in New York City. One senses that she appreciates basing her new business on Fifth Avenue as an extension of familiar surroundings.

Even though I've been covering the financial markets for 13 years, I've always wondered how others come into this business. At some point in their childhood, do they begin to plan to become fund managers? When do they get the "bug" to join the bustle of the street? Women haven't traditionally trained for this particular profession, and Liz would seem to fit the mold of women who took a circuitous route to the financial markets. As the daughter of a musician, she was not exposed to the world of finance. A career based on a liberal arts education would have seemed a more logical path for her.

Bramwell walked to her desk and motioned for me to take a seat. She took up a chair opposite me and began to quickly recount her early steps towards Wall Street. "I went to school on scholarships and graduated from Bryn Mawr College with a major in chemistry. I wasn't quite sure what I wanted to do after college. I knew I didn't want to go on and get a Ph.D. I just had too many other interests. At one point I thought I wanted to become a doctor, but the reality of spending that much time in school was depressing. I was ready to start my career. I had a friend in the Harvard/Radcliffe business program and another friend who gave me a subscription to the *Wall Street Journal*. I became increasingly interested in economics. I started taking courses at City College's Baruch School of Business at night. Then I enrolled in the Columbia Business School MBA program where I concentrated in finance, and from there I got a job at

Morgan Guaranty Trust Company in the investment research department. At Morgan I followed leisure time and specialty retailing stocks. At that time, banks were beginning to move from investing in very large cap stocks to smaller caps so I was presented with a great opportunity to analyze companies that had just gone public and where the founding entrepreneurs were often still in place. It was an exciting time."

At this point, Liz took an analyst's phone call. In 15 short minutes she asked very few but pointed questions and listened intently. Her questions were clipped and obviously well prepared, but not rapid-fire. She was keenly interested in the fundamentals—the comparison between the company in question and its competitors in regard to product and valuation. Quite honestly, I was hoping to hear her pepper the analyst with shrewd, probing questions. Instead, her queries were brief, presumably allowing the analyst room to provide as much information as possible without giving the analyst any indication of her reaction to the specifics.

After the call Liz picked right up where we left off, waxing enthusiastically about her career choice. Clearly she was having a good time. "I think we're in an extraordinary age where we can have more than one career. Wall Street is exciting because you are exposed to so much—from different industries to foreign cultures. Wall Street cuts across life and is a wonderful business for those who want to take a renaissance approach to learning and living. A liberal arts education is invaluable for a career on the Street. I think it's really important to study literature, history, different cultures, especially given the world we live in today. It's useful to know, for instance, the history behind the current political situation in Yugoslavia. If you know where people are coming from you can make better predictions on how they will react in the future. If you know the historic economic persuasions of the Federal Reserve Governors, then you have more insight into their next moves. If they are Keynesian economists as opposed to Chicago economists, their policies are likely to be quite different.

Wall Street is about more than understanding numbers: The 'numbers' will be meaningless if you don't have a sense of where they are coming from historically, politically, socially."

Liz started in the business in 1967 when Morgan had just named its first woman vice president, Dorothy "Dot" Connell—a major event at the time. Liz recognizes that she entered the fray when the bank was leading the pack in encouraging and promoting women. Some of her early experiences were delightfully amusing. Now a director of the New York Society of Security Analysts, Liz shared one of those early experiences: "When I first joined the bank I was asked to attend a lunch at the New York Society of Security Analysts, about two blocks from the office. My group head at the time asked me if I would be 'okay,' if I wouldn't prefer to have somebody go with me. It seems quaint now. About nine months later, I wanted to take a business trip to California to visit Mattel as the company looked like a promising investment. There was a bit of discussion on whether the bank should let a woman travel on her own. They did and a new paradigm was set."

Make no mistake about it, Liz is an unconventional woman and fund manager. She readily acknowledges that she challenges traditional approaches to finance, pointing out that the world is undergoing tremendous upheaval right now: Flexibility and the capacity to adapt to changing economic and sociological conditions are key to Liz's success. However, she has some very traditional views on mixing family and business. She stated quite clearly that she would not be starting her own business if she had young children (hers are in college now). When her second child was born, she took maternity leave from Bankers Trust and did not return. A year later, she went to work part-time for a hedge fund from one to three days a week. For the most part, although she kept a low profile in the business when her children were young, she does not feel that her gender held her back in any way and really doesn't spend much time thinking about the women versus men issue. "Women are women and men are men and it doesn't hurt to keep it that way," she said simply.

Liz's experience on Wall Street, long perceived as an exclusive men's club, would seem to indicate that the reality is drastically different from the perception. "People want performance and it's not dependent on gender—for anyone—in this country or elsewhere." While the Street may not be entirely gender neutral, being a woman has not affected Liz's ability to succeed. She is a firm believer in keeping the sexes separate, in not trying to be "one of the guys." No big fan of locker room language, Bramwell is intent on raising the level of professional conduct, not stooping to a lower level in an effort to fit in.

Liz steered the interview back to the markets. Perhaps slightly reticent about discussing her personal experiences, she was, however, enthusiastic about the markets. She is adept at thinking on her feet, a key skill in a dynamic financial landscape. Accordingly, she noted that "there's nothing wrong with changing your mind. You don't want to lock yourself into an opinion." Intellectually nimble, Liz is also almost rigidly disciplined in her approach to analysis, perhaps a result of her six years of studying Latin and training in the sciences.

"I think the market is a great deal more efficient today because of the speed of information and the ability we all now have to process it quickly. These two elements have always been part of the equation. Sometimes brokers have to make decisions without having all the pertinent information. We had more time to reflect in the past. On the up side, having quick access to historical records is very helpful; almost instantly we have a picture of a company over a long period of time and quick insight into competitors' histories as well."

As a part of the media that helps disseminate the information that the players seem to have an insatiable appetite for, I often wonder just how the experts sort through the seemingly endless data streams that bombard them from all sides. Liz acknowledged the challenge. "It's a major problem for everybody to sort out all the information. You clearly cannot read everything so an ability to discriminate is important. It used to be that the more information, the more efficient the markets. But now there is so much information that there are huge inefficiencies. For example, a brokerage house report will arrive that has been written a week ago—it's taken time to write it, print it, and mail it. So, a lot of people have had access to the information before it arrived on my desk. However, the market may not react for several days because everybody is focusing on something else, like the latest IPO (Initial Public Offering). There are real opportunities, if you can discern the important information from the superfluous.

"In terms of absorbing information, I believe in 'research grazing,' if you will. An hour's worth of reading at 6:00 A.M. without distractions can be more effective than two to three hours at a stretch after lunch, and quarterly reports fit very nicely into a handbag and can be read virtually anywhere."

But not all decisions are based exclusively on "the numbers." Whether it's professionals or individual investors making a buy or sell call, don't they just go with their gut feelings at a certain point? Doesn't intuition play a role in making the right calls?

Liz explained: "There are two types of analysis: quantitative and qualitative. You can analyze data and see, for example, that valuations look low when you apply various quantitative thresholds, but ultimately it comes down to qualitative judgment. For example, 'can this management handle 30 percent growth a year? Is the company gaining share or not?' The answers you're seeking are not necessarily going to show up in the quantitative numbers right away. The process is not exclusively intuitive, but informed opinions, developed from management interviews, presentations, and corporate reports—what they say, how they say it—and reading between the lines all play an important part in the decision making process."

Even though Liz made it clear that gender is not an issue in this business, she believes that women are more likely to have a sixth

sense—they are more comfortable adapting to changing information. More often than not, they can more easily make the jump from A to E without stopping off at B, C, and D. Ultimately, however, success for anyone, whether male or female, salesperson or company president, depends upon the ability to quickly process and prioritize a large number of changing variables.

Commenting on the brutal market pace, Liz said: "The momentum in today's financial marketplace is considerably accelerated. Technology has played a huge role in setting the new pace. It's hard to believe that calculators were once on the cutting edge of technology. When I started at the bank in 1967, we were still using slide rules! Calculators were just coming to market and they were huge—the size of most desktop computers today—and were kept in a special room. Can you believe that we operated without personal computers, doing all the work by hand? The business world was quite different then. Reaction time was slower and the work more meditative in nature. For example, we would manually keep track of the quarterly sales and earnings as they came out, as well as any changes in profit margins and tax rates. Today, with the click of a mouse, we can bring information onto the screen and readily see up-to-date historical data on an entire portfolio. But back in 1967, really not all that long ago, we had to crank out the analysis one stock at a time. Today's technology has made a tremendous difference in the flow of information. Changing brokerage house opinions about a given stock or corporate release can be pulled up on the screen instantly. One of the reasons for so-called momentum investing today is the ability to gain instant access to historical data to view the acceleration or deceleration in sales and earnings growth from one year to the next or sequentially."

Momentum, pace—this is a hyperkinetic business filled with intensely driven and competitive people. I wondered if Liz felt the industry is more competitive today than in, say, 1967. "The industry has definitely become much more competitive. A lot of people from the old school have retired from the business and the people who are in money management today are far more adept and driven than they were 30 years ago. It's a big market, even global, with a lot of choices and many new businesses have gone public in the last few years especially. This makes it more complex and also more intellectually challenging. Training new people in the business has changed and apprenticeship times have contracted. When I joined the bank, it took about five years to become a first level officer. Today that time has shrunk significantly to a year or so. Because of technology, the speed of writing reports and collecting and analyzing data has accelerated. Of course, judgment and interpretation are still paramount, but technology has facilitated the process."

Making the leap from successful fund manager to running one's own business is not a cut-and-dried process. Many just as successful as Liz have tried before and failed miserably—overwhelmed by the details of managing an office and staff. Balancing investment performance with internal operations can be an insurmountable challenge: One or the other inevitably seems to suffer, I noted. Liz agreed. "I found starting my own company a natural progression, however. If I were giving advice to someone starting out, I would recommend working for a large firm first where you can gain a lot of exposure to many different aspects of the business. You can always go from a big firm to a small one, but it's not so easy the other way around. Morgan Guaranty was a terrific place for me to start. There's a methodology there that's been arrived at over decades. Then I worked at William D. Witter as a sell-side analyst, focusing on specialty retailing, Disney, and a variety of other specific stocks. After that I returned to a bank investment department, namely Banker's Trust, concentrating on special situations—stocks the bank had not invested in historically. Next I worked with a hedge fund where the macroeconomic picture was *very* important. We spent a lot of time focusing on changes in interest and inflation rates and I went about picking stocks—opportunistically across industries. Finally, at Gabelli I was exposed to a private market value approach which is useful in certain markets.

"Starting off on my own, after such a wide range of experience, allows me to apply and integrate different methodologies to different situations. Applying fundamental analysis, looking at the big picture, using the private market value approach, and then amalgamating and improving from there, constantly evolving and changing, is the benefit and challenge of a broad background. It helps a financial manager see the whole picture."

Liz matter-of-factly explained that she had no trouble raising assets for her venture. The money pretty much just came to her, hardly surprising given her stellar reputation. Interestingly, however, the firm does not have a dedicated marketing person, and Liz likes it that way. It's hard to find a rainmaker who represents you accurately, and often when you hire rainmakers, you have to pull out an umbrella afterward.

I noticed during my tour of the office that Liz's staff is relatively small. As a result, each person's contribution is extremely important and visible. I asked her just how tough it had been to find a strong supporting cast. Liz smiled broadly. "I am fortunate to have a great staff. We have four MBAs, two of whom are Chartered Financial Analysts, who focus on research, plus a trader and administrator. Collectively, we have more than 75 years of investment industry experience. Additional technology and outsourcing permits us to provide services to our clients competitive with those of a much larger firm. For example, Advent software for portfolio management and trading takes the place of a large back office, allowing us to focus on investment rather than people management."

Liz works with outside vendors and went as far as interviewing six different organizations for custodian, transfer agent, and administrative services for The Bramwell Growth Fund. "We chose Firstar in Milwaukee because, among other things, they offered us a money market fund which means we didn't have to set one up ourselves. We also use Sunstone Financial in Milwaukee to do fund administration and fulfillment." The team's goal is to double the business over the next year. More importantly, they all seem to be enjoying themselves *now*—Liz especially. "Oh, I'm having a great time! I love making informed decisions and making things work more smoothly. Even little details are exciting, like acquiring a postage meter—no more guessing the postage! And on a bigger front, we are exploring opportunities on the Internet. It is truly gratifying to watch the firm grow and improve on all levels—from the individual team members to the office collectively."

And, finally, I love asking investment managers about their take on the future. This question always elicits a range of interesting responses—from the fantastic to the mundane. Liz's response seemed a mirror of her personality—highly observant, down-to-earth, to the point, yet flexible. "Change is increasingly rapid and continuous and in itself creates investment opportunities. Who knows what the future will bring, except that it will bring opportunities?"

The ability to adapt to a shifting market landscape has propelled Elizabeth Bramwell to the top of the game on Wall Street. It just may be the one character trait that will see her well into the next millennium.

Abby Joseph Cohen

Co-chair Investment Policy Committee, Goldman Sachs

On Wall Street, there are plum firms, and then there are *plum* firms. Goldman Sachs certainly exists somewhere at the top of the Street's food chain, a powerful, private partnership wielding tremendous influence in the global financial marketplace. Landing a position at Goldman, let alone an elusive, lofty partnership, is a career goal of untold numbers of men and women who flock to the Street every year. Few will realize that dream.

While not a partner (yet), Abby Joseph Cohen definitely holds a position of great power and influence at Goldman. If you had to construct a profile of a top Wall Street analyst and investment or stock market strategist, Abby would be the perfect model. She's got all the credentials: degrees in economics from Cornell University and George Washington University, a stint at the Federal Reserve Board in Washington D.C., and experience at big-name Wall Street firms, including T. Rowe Price and Drexel Burnham Lambert, culminating in her position at Goldman. She has not gotten to where she is by accident. Her work was a proven commodity long before she took up shop at Goldman.

Even by Wall Street standards, Abby Joseph Cohen lives and works at a breathless pace. It seemed like every time I tried to get in touch with her, she was out of the country. Because of this whirlwind schedule (she'd just flown back from London), we had to conduct our interview over the phone.

Getting an interview of this sort with Abby is no small task. Besides scheduling issues, there is also the fact that Goldman closely guards its operations and reputation: One of the firm's public relations representatives was required to sit in on the interview, for the most part a silent, but still noticeable, presence throughout the call.

Abby comes across as either unaffected or unimpressed by the obstacles that often confront women on the Street. Perhaps she has always been too absorbed in her work (and too good at it) to be distracted by politics of any sort. She chose her path because she was looking for an "intellectual challenge," and she doesn't seem to be a woman who is easily challenged. One can imagine Abby addressing problems in business in much the same way she must approach the markets: as a series of problems to be analyzed and solved. Given her responsibilities and the deftness with which she executes them, it's not surprising that Abby seems all business.

Abby is one of the few women I've talked to who seem as though they were meant for life on the Street; her background seemed to point her squarely in that direction, although she doesn't really think so herself. While many other women studied liberal arts or science in college and found themselves on the Street almost by accident, Abby had a hard-core economic background. It's true she didn't actively seek out a Wall Street job; as it turned out, the Street sought *her* out.

"Well, for me it was a little serendipitous," Abby said. "I started out with training in economics, and I was an economist with the Fed in Washington, working on issues that were relevant to the financial markets. I received a phone call from T. Rowe Price, who asked me, 'How would you like to do what you're doing for the Fed, but for an investment firm?' It sounded very interesting to me."

Her experience at the Federal Reserve Bank certainly distinguished Abby. In a way, her presence there was as notable as the presence of the first women on the Street. But, she was able to learn a great deal and seems to have nothing but positive memories.

"The Fed was wonderful, it's really a fabulous organization," she recalled. "In Washington, they probably have the world's largest gathering of professional economists. It's a great environment—very professional, very intellectual. It was an excellent place to use my economics training to work on real-world issues. Among the projects to which I was assigned was helping re-work the Fed's inflation forecasting model." She gave a little chuckle. "This was in the 1970s, so inflation was of course a critical issue at the time. I also worked on other projects having to do with banking."

Abby was one of a few women working at the Fed in those days, although she stresses she was only one of a number of women who were beginning to make an impact on that organization. "It was a generational thing," she said. "There were certainly a larger number of women in my age category than in the older categories, so we were the vanguard in terms of being the first large group of women academically trained in economics and beginning to move through the ranks."

Looking back, Abby doesn't see many disadvantages or advantages in being a woman in that environment during that period. It may have been somewhat more progressive than the Street in rewarding performance. "I don't think it was an asset," she said flatly. "But I don't think it was a liability, either. At the Fed, what you were asked to do and your chances of promotion were merit-oriented."

Although she enjoyed her three-year stay at the Fed, Abby's decision to leave was eventually prompted by the feeling that her upward progress was limited in that organization's existing hierarchy. She saw greener pastures in the world of smaller, private sector companies. When T. Rowe Price called, she was ready to move. When I asked her if she saw a lack of meritocracy when she made the move to Wall Street, she laughed a little, answering quickly, "I don't have any complaints. When I look at the responsibilities I've been given at Goldman Sachs, I like to think it's on the basis of merit, and that my 'leaders' have decided I have the ability to handle them."

Although she's hesitant to speak for any other person or group on the Street, Abby's experience has been that Wall Street is generally "gender-neutral"—as long as you perform well and satisfy the clients. Make money, you're in; don't, and you're out. "My feeling about the two firms I've spent most of my time with, Drexel and now Goldman Sachs, was that they were interested in getting the job done," she claimed. "It's really a matter of necessity. In any firm that is interested in number one, serving the client, and number two, making a profit, you want to put the right people in the right slots. You don't have enough margin for error that you can say, 'Well, I'll put somebody less-qualified in this slot because they fit the following nonrelevant criteria.' You really want to go with the person who can do the best job."

Abby spent approximately eight years at T. Rowe Price. Although she was using many of the same skills she had at the Fed, she was now applying them from an entirely different perspective. Her economic and computer training proved to be the perfect background for a time when technology and financial engineering were really coming into their own.

"I started out as an economist," she remembered. "Keep in mind that I had come from the Fed where I was involved in analyzing current business conditions and building computer models; I was brought into T. Rowe Price to do the same thing, but from the standpoint of helping their investment process. Then I shifted to a related responsibility: I became the so-called 'quant' [quantitative analyst]. New approaches such as modern portfolio theory and quantitative analysis are, in my view, just applied economics. In the late '70s and early '80s many investment firms were discovering that some extraordinary things could be done by applying computer models, better databases, and so on. My background made me well-suited for that."

The application of these new technologies resulted in a sea change in the way investment houses did business, and Abby found it exciting. "Some people would say it was a quantum leap forward, cynics would say it was a half-step back, but the industry was moving from a more qualitative, seat-of-the-pants approach to investment management to something that was much more disciplined. It was very satisfying to be part of the process because we were trying to understand how portfolios were best constructed, understand and measure the risks that were implicit in them, understand the tilts and biases—the bets that were being made in the portfolio—and for the first time in history, we truly had the tools to do that."

Although she seems as self-sufficient a person as you could meet on the Street, Abby does cite two people who stood out in terms of influencing her career. "One person I would point to is Burt Siegel, who was research director at Drexel," she said. "He plucked me from the 'buy side' of the street and said, 'We want you to do something a little more dramatic.' He felt that investment strategy could be enhanced by using the new tools and techniques. Instead of someone sitting on the mountain top and pontificating about things, he thought results would be improved by a more disciplined approach. He hired me to combine economics with quantitative analysis with the goal of building investment strategies. He was very supportive that investment strategy could be done in this manner, and gave me the opportunity to do it." The second influence was Steve Einhorn, who, not surprisingly, hired Abby at Goldman Sachs.

"To be a principle spokesperson on the market outlook for a firm like Goldman is quite a flattering position to be in," she noted.

At Drexel, Abby was able to expand her horizons; she had a great deal of computer and research resources at her disposal. She did, however, make a point of distinguishing between the equity division, where she worked, and the more notorious West Coast bond division. She characterized the work she and her colleagues did as high quality, professional, and consistently ranked among the leaders in their field. Nonetheless, she received her pink slip, like so many others, when Drexel unraveled in 1990. "It was a character-building experience," she said. "It was interesting to see where people ended up. Almost everybody from the equity research department quickly landed jobs elsewhere in the business. It was considered to be such a high-quality department, all these people were in great demand." After a brief stint at the British firm Barclays de Zoete Wedd, Abby made the move to Goldman Sachs in 1990. She's been there ever since.

I commented that it didn't appear that she ran into many prejudices as she moved up through the ranks. It was difficult to tell if she really hadn't noticed prejudices or if she was just keeping a stiff upper lip. "I don't think there was anything really overt," Abby answered in measured tones. "I could obviously give you a few anecdotes here or there, but I don't know that they had an enormous impact on my life."

When asked if she could single out any personal traits that contributed to her success, Abby thought about it a moment and said, "I try to ignore the noise. When people are panicking or running for the exits, I try to take a careful look and be analytical. One of the keys to success is objectivity: Don't get caught up in the daily flow of market news or gossip or who's doing what today; focus on the long-term. The work I do is very much fundamentally driven: what's really going on in the economy, what's really going on in corporations and individuals' investment trends. It's been very helpful to focus longer-term than most other people do. I think it keeps us more stable and consistent and helps us be right on our market views over the intermediate to longer-term. The *Wall Street Journal* runs a survey that has ranked our portfolio strategy as the best from the major brokerage firms for the last five years."

Abby talked a little bit about how the tendency of most people to get caught up in the news presents opportunities for those able to take a step back and look at things dispassionately. "In 1990, I had done a lot on long-term cycles in the U.S. and I came up with a few conclusions: One, inflation was still likely to move lower; two, government spending as a percentage of GDP was likely to move lower; three, the aging of the baby boom generation would mean a movement into savings and investments, muting consumption spending. Also, I realized corporations had become much more cautious, managing better and focusing on the bottom line.

"Those conclusions seem obvious now, but they didn't seem so obvious then. But by doing our homework properly, we've been able to get through some significant but transitory rough patches in the market and say, 'Wait a minute, we realize things may be disappointing this month, but the long-term pattern is still quite good.' If you've got the three- to five-year outlook right, it helps you live through some of the near-term disappointments."

But Abby pointed out that she's also flexible; she's been bearish before, having noticed signs in 1990 that indicated a recessionary environment. When there's any doubt, she goes back to basics and tries to determine if there's anything wrong with the materials she's working with—the computer model or the data she's using, for example. "The other point to remember is what Keynes said: 'When the facts change, I change my mind. What do you do?' There have been several times in my professional life when I've stood up and said, 'Okay, I didn't get that one right, here's why,' and then I'll restart. One problem many people face is a reluctance to admit mistakes. I think it's much healthier to thoroughly examine every-thing, admit when you've made an error, and start over with a clean slate."

Although Abby said she doesn't use any "gut feeling" in her analysis per se, she and her colleagues must step back and try to de-termine how the economic facts may be interpreted, or misinter-preted, by investors. "It's always important to assess the difference be-tween economic reality and investor perception, because the markets should be driven by reality on an intermediate to long-term basis, but they can be driven by perception in the short-term. You have to figure out whether the current investor perception is right or wrong."

Like many others in the business, Abby is of the opinion that Wall Street employs some of the most innovative and exceptional minds around. Research analysis, particularly, depends on creativity. Abby is pleased with the amount of latitude she now has. "In my current position, we're encouraged to be thoughtful and creative. If not in research, where are you going to find that?"

For now, Abby is understandably very happy doing what she's doing. "My job is to think about broad trends in the market and how our clients can benefit from that at all different levels. I find it intel-lectually stimulating, but I also enjoy meeting and working with so many different people."

But, there's still a downside. Despite her composure and profes-sional demeanor, Abby is not oblivious to the stress and workload that comes with a position like hers. "Sometimes the travel is very difficult," she conceded. "We have clients all over the world, so I might have to go to Europe, Asia, Australia—not to mention all over the United States. This is a big continent, you know," she added wryly.

Although Abby was very reluctant to discuss personal matters, she said, surprisingly, that balancing her career with a family has not been particularly difficult, something she credits to the support of her husband, and two daughters. She noted that her husband had a professional mother and so perhaps was more prepared to have a wife that didn't follow a conventional path. Abby's parents simply presumed that a high-level career was in the offing and provided encouragement and enthusiasm.

Abby is very highly regarded on the Street. She laughed a little when I brought up the subject of partnership. "I'm very pleased with the internal recognition I have received. I am treated with the utmost respect and am given a great deal of responsibility—I feel very appreciated." She was also quick to give credit to her coworkers, often referring to the work "we" do or the calls "we" made.

Talking about some of the conspicuous moments in her career, Abby singled out the work she and her Goldman colleagues performed early in the decade when they bucked a prevailing trend of bearishness toward the U.S. economy and financial markets. "We felt it was unwarranted, which presented a wonderful investment opportunity. Again, it's that gap between perception and reality. Everyone thought the U.S. was growing slowly, that corporations had big problems, government spending was out of control. Yet, we felt very strongly there were a number of notable points of inflection and substantive changes in the winds. I'm very pleased to have analyzed that correctly and to have recognized that it would be a long-lasting phenomenon.

"The other call I'm proud of was made the day after the crash in October 1987, saying to our clients, 'This is a great opportunity for stocks and bonds.' It was one of those cases of 'ignoring the noise,' looking at what was a traumatic market event and recognizing 'this is not going to have a notable economic impact,' that the economy was in reasonably good condition, and that stocks were inexpensive based on any thoughtful outlook for 1988 earnings. We suggested to clients that they be heavily involved in stocks and bonds."

In the past few years, Abby has further enhanced her position on the Street by becoming more involved in various industry organizations. She's concerned about setting standards and raising the level of professional conduct in the investment industry. She finds the time to do this, because of "all that time on airplanes," she joked. "I have been most interested in the educational efforts in the investment community. I believe that the proper functioning of the capital markets worldwide is going to depend on whether investors understand what they're doing. There's an organization in our industry called the Institute for Chartered Financial Analysts of which I am the chair this year. It runs a detailed educational program for professional investors. About 30,000 people around the world prepared for this year's exams by reading thousands of pages and studying for hundreds of hours. I'm really proud to be involved in the CFA program because good training is of great importance to the future of the investment industry. People might have come into the investment community decades ago with little preparation, but now they need very specific training in economics, finance theory, mathematics, and valuation. The CFA program also stresses a high standard of ethics.

"The industry worldwide is coming closer together from a professional standpoint. The success of the CFA study program is exciting because it reflects an industry-wide acknowledgment that professional and ethical standards must be maintained globally. There has to be a basic level of competency for people who assume the responsibility of managing other people's money."

Abby would do it all again, but she did have a word of caution, both for her industry and people thinking of entering it. "I was looking for a career that would be stimulating, and it has been, because what I do changes from week to week—the issues change, the industry itself changes—so for me it's has been very exciting. What I wonder about though, is whether some of the people who are now flocking to the industry view it as just another job, or a way to earn an above-average income. Many people are going to be disappointed, because unless you really enjoy it, live and breathe it, it can become very taxing: long hours, long-term commitment, and there's also volatility in the structure of this industry. Unless you're getting a 'psychic challenge' from this profession, it can be very wearying."

For now, Abby certainly seems to be weathering the storm, and then some. She's a face on the Street that bears continued watching.

Elizabeth Mackay

Chief Investment Strategist and Managing Director,
Bear Stearns

I was having one of those urban experiences that makes even the most die-hard concrete fan consider moving to a small town in Idaho. I was headed out to interview Liz Mackay and had just finished circling the Bear Stearns building for the seventh time in my car when I realized that there was no way I would find a place to park at this hour. What had I expected? It was rush hour in New York—traffic was bumper to bumper. As I kept looking at my watch, I could feel my blood pressure pushing into the red zone. After about 25 minutes, by some miracle I found an opening in a parking lot a couple of blocks away in the Diamond District. In New York, you take what you can get.

I stepped out of my car and was immediately engulfed in a noisy, colorful swirl of humanity: Hasidic Jews wearing long back robes and top hats, suit-clad men and women clutching briefcases and purses, hurrying to catch trains, kids hawking late-edition newspapers, and police in dark blue coats, blasting their whistles as they waved and urged the endless stream of cars through the intersections.

I walked quickly, zigzagging between waves of shoppers and commuters, trying to ignore the rows of enticing shop windows glinting with countless gems. Only my appointment with Liz and my empty pocketbook kept me on my chosen course. In the midst of that tempting street, I thought, *Why the hell did I park here?*

I finally arrived, exhausted, at her building, took the elevator up to her floor, and waited briefly in the lobby. Elizabeth waltzed in and embraced me with a businesslike hug. As we walked down a seemingly endless maze of corridors to her office, I had the impression of being in a massive corporate labyrinth. *I'm going to need some help getting out of here,* I thought.

This wasn't the first time I'd had the pleasure of seeing Liz. Just a few weeks before, she had been in the CNBC studio wearing a bright red suit with faux fir trim. "It's imitation leopard," she had informed me with a smile. Television people love Liz. A visual delight, she looks great on camera, has a lovely, resonant broadcast voice, and gives a great sound bite. She looked, I noticed, as fantastic as ever, decked out in a snazzy royal blue Chanel suit with gold buttons.

New York is filled with women and men who spend a great deal of money and time on their appearance, desperately trying to convince others (and perhaps themselves) that they are *somebody,* on their way to *somewhere.* Elizabeth Mackay, while stylish as anyone in Manhattan, has already arrived: At the relatively young age of 38, she is one of Wall Street's most successful women, chief investment strategist and managing director at Bear Stearns. "Come on in and make yourself at home," she said in her familiar broadcast voice, ushering me into her office.

For a moment, this looked easier said than done. The room was overflowing with stacks of magazines and other reading material encompassing everything from foreign affairs to oil production. Journals and piles of newsletters filled every inch of her office, leaving barely enough room for a desk and two chairs.

At Bear Stearns, which has long had a reputation of being a fairly competitive shop, positions like Liz's are highly coveted. As Liz reflected on her rapid ascent, it was apparent that this is a woman who goes after what she wants without hesitation. "I first interviewed with a headhunter who sent me to Bear Stearns for a round of interviews, but nothing came of that. She may have felt I was too young and lacked credibility. I remember saying to a colleague about that time, 'Do I really want a job at Bear Stearns?' 'Yes, I think you do,' he replied. 'Why? Have they offered you a job?' 'No, but I'm sure I can get one if I want to,' I answered. Soon after, I heard Larry Kudlow at Bear Stearns speak at a luncheon. A day or two later, I wrote a strategy piece on the market and sent it to him with a note: 'Larry, this is the kind of work I do; I think it would dovetail with your economics work.' I followed up with a call and after several more interviews ended up landing the job. I've never looked back."

While her latest focus is domestic financial markets, it wasn't always so. Liz had "gone global" long before the term became trendy on Wall Street, her international perspective manifesting itself at an early age. I'd heard a story circulating on the Street that when Liz was a teenager she sought out a high school that taught Russian and talked her parents into letting her attend. I asked her if this was true.

Liz gave me a mischievous half-smile. "It's true that I used to tell my school friends, 'You know, Russian could be a great language to know somewhere down the road.' That became a standing joke in the office when I first started on the Street. Some of the guys at Merrill used to laugh and say, 'Hey Liz, that Russian's pretty useful on Wall Street. When Merrill opens a Moscow branch, they're sure

to make you manager!' But it's not so funny anymore. It's very interesting how the world has changed—I think most of those guys who
laughed back then are now out of the business," she mused.

Shortly after Liz graduated from college, with no job prospects
in sight, she put her steely resolve to work. A self-starter with a gam-
bler's nerve, Liz called an options firm she had read about in the *Wall
Street Journal* and asked for a job. "Do you know anything about options?" the firm's personnel manager inquired. "Of course," she said
confidently. Her next phone call was to a friend who worked on
Wall Street: "What's an option?"

Liz continued to be aggressive in the face-to-face meeting. "I
was invited in for an interview and the president of the company
challenged me, 'You can't really have much knowledge of options.
Your resume says that you're a psychology major. What makes you
think you can do this job?' I learned forward in my chair, looked
him in the eye, and replied simply, 'I can do anything I want to.' He
flopped back in his chair, picked up the telephone, dialed his partner, and said, 'This is the question I asked her, and listen to what she
said.' He held the phone out and had me repeat myself. Having the
mindset that I can do anything got me that job. Also, ironically, being a woman and looking relatively young helped along the way
because the expectation level was lower—it was easier to excel and
impress."

Six months later, Liz joined Merrill Lynch in the Market Analysis Department. "I was so lucky," Liz said. "I worked with the legendary Bob Farrell for seven years. I had just entered the Street and
decided to attend classes at the New York Institute of Finance to
broaden my understanding of the business (the options firm had sent
me to this class) and I asked one of my instructors, Ralph Acampora,
if he knew anyone in the business looking for help. He told me that
a guy by the name of Bob Farrell over at Merrill Lynch was looking
for someone to keep charts for him. He said, 'Look, if you have to
sweep the floor, do it; just get into Merrill.' Bob Farrell is the person

responsible for Wall Street firms adopting technical analysis. His name is gold at Merrill."

Liz spent her first seven years as a technical analyst with Merrill. "If I had realized at the time how big Bob was, how big this whole business is, I probably would have blown the first interview. That job turned out to be the best experience I could have gotten anywhere. Every morning we had general meetings, and I was constantly impressed by the top-notch people in attendance. I felt so lucky to be a part of that team. Then, as the years went on, I became more and more interested in what was *behind* the bars on the charts."

I had been told that Liz has both an insatiable desire for new challenges and an unusual ability to process mountains of information. Her cluttered office belied one of her secrets. "I read everything I can on almost any subject," she explained. The head-high piles of books, magazines, and reports surrounding us made this more than an idle boast.

Elizabeth brushed back a sweep of reddish-blond hair and admitted, "I have to tell you, honestly, I basically fell into my career. I had been a psychology major in college, and I knew I couldn't do much in psychology without a master's degree or Ph.D. When I graduated from college with a B.A., I decided to do something else for a while, and planned to return later for my master's in psychology.

"Meanwhile, Wall Street sounded interesting. I like money and there's no master's degree in Wall Street, per se. But everything happens quickly in options, and I soon figured out that wasn't what I wanted to do. I like to process information, I like to overprepare. I'm not a seat-of-the-pants person, and options trading is the consummate seat-of-the-pants business. But I was lucky to find a niche I loved."

When I asked Liz how her clients react to her being a woman, she looked at me closely and said, "Well, one of my male clients just told me the other day, 'Liz, I love the idea of having a female strategist for the same reason my accountant is a woman and my lawyer is a woman. For a woman to attain a high level in a male-dominated profession, she has to work twice as hard and/or be twice as smart.' Other male clients have also expressed support. One of the biggest said, 'Liz, it's not about gender, it's about you making me money, and you do that well.' "

After a pause I asked Liz if the business has always been as cut-throat as it is today. She shook her head and sighed. "No. It has always been competitive, but today it's even worse. Every other firm has downsized. I guess it's no different than any enterprise where the stakes are in the millions, or any business that offers what people greedily aspire to: fame and money. When chairs are removed and the music stops, some people are not going to have a seat. That increases the competitive element and the pressure. However, if you have the goods, you'll most likely be the one to get that seat."

When I asked her how she became one of those people "with the goods," she credited her early years at Merrill Lynch. What did she find particularly rewarding about the experience? "It was the chance to be creative," she explained. "There's always room on Wall Street for new ideas, new approaches, and Merrill Lynch was the perfect vehicle. Merrill was great from a people point of view, too. It was a new firm, with lots of different types of people and personalities to learn from. Right next door to me was the fixed-income department, which I didn't know anything about yet, then there was the trading floor. There were so many facets to the business that the potential seemed endless. It inspired me to keep growing and applying myself.

"It was a fabulous place to work. The first day I walked into Merrill Lynch, it was an instant perfect fit. I remember Bob assuring me that being a psychology major would prove an ideal background for a market analyst. He immediately saw unlimited possibilities for me, so I could too," she said with obvious appreciation.

Despite her contentment at Merrill Lynch, one day Elizabeth got an offer she couldn't refuse. "Was it hard to leave?" I asked. "Very hard," Liz replied, "but I had been doing technical analysis for a while and wanted to try something new. I had sent my resume to Brown Brothers Harriman and got a call from Tom Campbell, the head of portfolio management there. After several interviews, I did the hardest thing I've ever had to do in my career: I told Bob Farrell I was leaving. We both had tears in our eyes, but he confided, 'I don't blame you. It's a terrific opportunity.' "

I ask Liz if she thought she'd made the right decision, knowing that she had subsequently worked at Brown Brothers for five years. She was their investment strategist with the chairman of the investment policy committee, and three years of the five, she actively managed portfolios.

"It was fabulous because I learned about economics, and fixed income and portfolio management. I absorbed it all like a sponge. Working at Brown Brothers opened up a whole new world for me because they were very big on watching what the Federal Reserve was doing," Liz said. "About halfway through my tenure there, the head of the investment policy committee became the head of the asset management side of the firm. I walked into his office and said, 'I've always wanted to manage money,' and he said, 'Okay, go for it,' after endless discussions and repeated harassment. Basically, that's how I began. I managed mostly individuals' money, and I continued doing that for about three years. To a great degree, a money manager manages relationships as much as money. It was challenging in terms of bringing something new to the table.

"Also, it was complicated to keep in touch with the big picture—stay updated, manage portfolios, perform stock analysis—plus deal with clients. Having good relationships with clients helps. If people like you, they'll overlook it if you goof a little. A turning point for me happened just before the Gulf War, during Desert Shield, when the markets collapsed. I'd only had my clients for about four months then. I had enough background in interest rates and oil to tell each one clearly what was happening, and why, and what to expect. That really boosted their confidence in me and I feel they really became *my* clients during that period."

Those who have met Liz Mackay know her as well-spoken, very giving and open, with a wonderful sense of humor—someone who is always ready to laugh. One doesn't expect this sweetness and thoughtfulness in such a busy Wall Street professional. She's a grounded, generous presence in a business that sometimes produces, or rewards, hypercompetitive, high-strung personalities.

Liz's proverbial wall of strength? Her parents. They encouraged the adventuresome spirit which eventually enabled Liz to make it on the Street. Liz reflected, "I was absolutely blessed with supportive parents. Anything I am, I owe to my parents. They gave me the biggest gift a parent can give a child: Confidence. I simply don't have a fear of failure. I've always had a tendency to be very bold in terms of getting up and taking a chance."

Everyone who saw the movie *Wall Street* came away with the impression that the Street is made up of cold and uncaring salesmen without a creative bone among them. But talking to Liz reinforced my belief that the movie misrepresented the Street and the people who work there—in fact, you *have* to be creative in order to be successful. When I voiced these thoughts to Liz she declared, "Exactly! In fact, I think it's one of the most creative places to work on earth. If you aren't creative, you don't survive. Sometimes you have to come up with an earthshaking new idea every week."

While Wall Street may offer women the chance to achieve a level of power and prestige unattainable in other fields, such opportunity does not come without a price. Rather than facing a choice between a career and a life as a wife or mother, women today are often obliged to do all three—on a full-time basis. I thought briefly about how hard it's been for me, trying to grow professionally with a husband in medical school. I asked Liz how she balances a full-time career and a marriage.

"My husband and I have been married 12 years," she replied. "He's also in the business, and we both often wind up working all weekend. He understands what I go through. I don't know if someone outside of Wall Street could understand the pressures. Another person might think, *Oh, what's the big deal? The market's dropped 50 points; so you made a mistake, so what?* He has experienced personally what I go through. Sometimes I think both of us being in the business is a plus—maybe not a plus in terms of being overworked, but another person's experience helps you achieve better balance and a more accurate perspective. On the other hand, you can get so involved in Wall Street that you forget there's a world outside."

I changed the subject, asking her how much time she spends doing research. She replied, "I'm *constantly* doing research. The weekend is spent reading the *Economist,* the *Washington Post,* et cetera. I really can't read enough. I don't get a chance to read the trade journals as often as I would like to." Liz advises institutional investment clients and the retail sales force on market trends, asset allocation, and specific investment themes by considering a wide variety of fundamental economic, political, international, and technical variables, so she needs to get information from a wide variety of sources.

Listening to Liz discuss the importance of communicating effectively, I was somewhat surprised (and flattered) to hear her say that I was one of her role models. "One year when I was at Merrill, I was constantly sick with sinus infections," Liz remembered. "I would watch you, Sue, on TV and think, 'That woman is so composed, has such natural charisma.' Oprah Winfrey had just started her show, and she, too, seemed so in control. In this business, you've got to be able to present yourself well and role models are important."

It's been said that if you follow your passion, the money will follow. But if you chase the almighty dollar, you can easily lose that, and then end up with nothing. Liz has followed her passion, and as a result, she is happy and fulfilled. As she said, "My best clients look for somebody who will make them think. You may not necessarily be right, but if you introduce an idea that your clients haven't thought of before and that makes them see a new dimension, you are highly valued. I've always thought that being an instant guru is not something to aspire to, because it's so temporary. I want to be known as somebody who consistently does good, thoughtful work. I think that's how you can endure on Wall Street, rather than becoming just a flash in the pan. Success is about doing what is most valuable to you.

"Writing is something else I enjoy, another creative avenue in my life," Liz added. "Sometimes I think to myself, *Here's a blank piece of paper. I can put anything I want on it. I can discuss any aspect of the market environment, or talk about a specific industry, or the political situation.* It's extremely rewarding when things come together—when the chart looks one way and the fundamentals seem to support that, plus there's legislation pending, or something in the political scene that supports the direction you foresee. That's very gratifying."

Although Liz has risen to a fairly lofty position, no job ever seems to be secure on the Street. Liz seems to be in a very male, very competitive environment, even by the standards of the Street. I wondered if she still felt pressure and asked her if it was true that Bear Stearns is a cutthroat, high-testosterone workplace.

"Whether Bear Stearns or Wall Street in general, I'd have to say not so much today as 16 years ago," Liz replied, "but the old boys' club still dominates. However, if you can quantify what you do, that readily removes the discrimination factor. In that sense, Wall Street is probably a better place, relative to some others, for women. If you're good, if you've got the goods, you'll be compensated. It's all about performance." She seemed to reflect for a moment. "Women actually do quite well on Wall Street because so much of this business is intuitive. Being good at this often involves being able to see or piece things together that aren't obvious. Women are also less likely to have their egos tied up in their decisions, and therefore are more able to reverse direction if necessary."

I asked Liz for any advice she might have for women in the workplace. She thought about it for a moment and responded, "I'd say you have to have a sense of humor in life and business. Two weeks ago, I took a client in to see one of my colleagues. When I left the room, my fellow analyst blew kisses at me. I could have run to the research director and said, 'Listen to what he did! He undermined my status and credibility with this client.' But the client had a sense of humor. Bottom line: life's short and you've got to pick your battles; it's better to laugh something like this off. The good news for women interested in working in the financial field is that at entry level there is much less discrimination—but as you move up, that element surfaces. It's often simply an undercurrent of the question, *Will she leave to have children?* You can't legislate attitudes or fears. A man is still much more secure in terms of tenure."

As I slowly navigated my way out of her building and back through the Diamond District, I came away feeling that Elizabeth Mackay's future on the Street is very much secure. Very few women have accomplished what she has with so few scars to show for it. Her star hangs above Wall Street like a beacon, encouraging other women to follow her lead, bravely take up the challenge, and, as Liz might say—have the confidence to use their impressive powers of insight and intuition.

As for me, I had trouble enough making my way back to my car.

Muriel Siebert

Muriel Siebert & Co.

On one of the few sunny days of the most brutal New York winter in memory, I bounced in a cab up Fifth Avenue on my way to meet with Muriel Siebert at her upper-east-side digs. To prepare for our interview, I began to run through her long list of accomplishments in my mind.

It's almost impossible to separate the word "first" from this woman: the first woman to buy a seat on the New York Stock Exchange, the first female owner of a New York Stock Exchange brokerage firm, one of the first discount brokers, the first female banking superintendent of New York State—even the first female member of the Wings Club. (When I asked her at one point why she thought more was written about her than any other woman on Wall

Street, she answered matter-of-factly, "For a long time, there was nobody else, period.")

While such firsts have typically been the focus of the numerous interviews and stories about her over the years, they are merely the most conspicuous milestones of a career that has less to do with ends than means—how she lives her life and what she stands for, rather than the accolades or material rewards that may distinguish her in the eyes of the casual observer. Muriel is understandably proud of her role in opening up the corridors of power on the Street to a new generation of women, and she seems to take her position as a patron of women's causes seriously. But for her, this role was not initially a conscious choice, but rather the inevitable outcome of her drive to succeed in her chosen profession—a business she loved.

I thought about my own career. It wasn't too long ago that television broadcasting, like Wall Street, was an exclusively male stronghold, and the fledgling female newscasters of the '60s and '70s were almost considered novelties—a nod to social fashion, or a cynical attempt to grab ratings. Even now, women have to scrap continually to command respect in this industry. I wondered what it must have been like for a true pioneer like Muriel Siebert—a woman for whom there was no precedent.

I got answers to some of my questions as I sat down to breakfast with Muriel in the River Club adjacent to her exclusive River House address, home to more than a few well-heeled New Yorkers, Henry Kissinger among them. The elegant surroundings—high ceilings, richly paneled walls, glinting chandeliers, warm fireplaces, and big bay windows offering a beautiful view of the East River—hark back to a more civilized, glamorous Manhattan. It was, I realized, the perfect setting in which to discuss the past and future of the Street with a woman who has both shaped and been shaped by that legendary slice of U.S. business culture.

While she can regale you with more than her fair share of stories from a bygone era of the Street, Muriel is hardly living in the past. She is firmly focused on the future and is as irreverent, energetic, controversial, and outspoken as ever. At an age (63) when many men and women are considering where to spend their retirement, Muriel is in the midst of expanding her business, the discount brokerage and underwriter Muriel Siebert & Company, and widening her philanthropic endeavors, including her support of women's businesses and political campaigns. All the while, she brushes off the slings and arrows of her naysayers—some of whom have suggested she should concentrate on choosing a successor rather than continuing to hold the reins herself—with the same confidence she has for over 40 years.

Perhaps not surprisingly for a woman who had to blaze her own trail, Muriel's path was not a straight line, but rather a series of twists and turns. Hers is a story of a woman who was often in the right place at the right time: a euphemism, really, for the talent of seeing opportunity where no one else does, and making the most of it.

We settled down in the dining room and ordered breakfast. As we stirred our coffee and waited for our omelets to arrive, I asked her to tell me a little about the early days, about what drew her to Wall Street. She took a sip of coffee before she answered.

"I dropped out of college [Case Western Reserve in her hometown of Cleveland] when my father was dying of cancer," she recalled. "I cut classes and played bridge because I just couldn't stand what I was seeing at home, and at some point I just lost interest and never went back. My mother was the youngest of 11 children, and my Uncle Ben was the oldest; his son was a U.N. representative, so I went to New York and applied for a job at the U.N. because I thought it looked interesting. But I didn't speak two languages, so the U.N. was out.

"But," she continued, "I had been to New York once before and I had taken a bus tour of the city, and one of the stops was the Stock Exchange. I had a feeling about it—I thought it looked exciting—

but I really only expected to stay three or four months and then go home. So, I applied to Merrill Lynch because they were the biggest. They asked me if I had a college degree and I said no. That was that. Then I applied at Bache the next day and when they asked me if I had a college degree, I said yes!" Muriel laughed a little at the recollection. "They offered me $65 a week as a trainee in research, or $75 a week in their bookkeeping department. I took the research position. I have a talent: I can look at a page of numbers and they light up and tell me a story."

That doesn't really seem like a fast-track position. How were you able to distinguish yourself?

"When I started, Bache was expanding—they only had six or seven analysts—and every analyst was given the opportunity to dump an industry on a new trainee. So the analyst who had railroads, shipping, airlines, buses—everything that moved—gave me airlines." Muriel paused for a moment and looked at me to convey the enormity of this stroke of fortune. "This was an old railroad guy who knew every inch of the railroads and felt that airlines were taking up too much of his time, so I got airlines! Another analyst whose area was primarily chemicals and drugs, also had radio, television, and motion pictures—they were his little side industry that he had to cover. So he dumped those on me, and I wrote the first study of the Value of the Depreciated Films for Television. Then I started covering aerospace because of my knowledge of the airlines, and both those industries turned hot. That movie depreciation report and the value of the libraries helped put me on the map. It was the first time something like it had been done. It forced people to think: 'What are these companies worth?' "

Having honed her research skills and solidified her reputation, Muriel moved on to another brokerage, Shields & Company, where she got her first taste of doing stock orders. "I actually got my first order there by accident," she remembered. "One day a fund manager called and said, 'We made money on a report you wrote, we owe you an order.' So I went to the partner in charge of research and asked if I should wait until I got registered, and he practically shoved me out the door, saying, 'You get the order, we'll make it up to you at Christmas time.' So, I started to make pretty good money by doing orders."

Were men at the company jealous? I asked. Did they treat you any differently, or were you just one of the guys? I mentioned to Muriel that Bernadette Murphy told me that she kind of felt like one of the guys because they started calling her "Murphy" and "Murph."

"Well, the analysts always treated me as one of the guys, the companies always treated me as one of the guys—I mean, the aviation companies loved me—I became the first woman member of the Wings Club. But some of the 'secure' people on the Street aren't that secure. I realized that people like things status quo. It wasn't against me. It took me two years to realize that it wasn't personal, it was just that I was breaking the status quo: 'What are we going to do? How can we send her to hear this company at lunch when they don't accept women at the luncheon club.' "

That actually occurred? I asked, surprised. How did you work around that? "Sometimes I couldn't," Muriel said flatly. "Sometimes they sent a man. Some of those things still weren't done at that time. But, I still learned to sell stocks, which was pretty remarkable because I used to stutter, you know—I wasn't a salesperson.

"We had a good group at Shields, though. One guy there stood up for me at a certain point when I started to look for another job because I was hired at $9,500, approximately 40 percent less than the men. He went to the partners and said, 'She's looking for a job. It's not fair.' I had left Bache for the same reason—they were paying the men more. You know, there's a big difference when you're making $130 a week and the men are making $200. That's a 'quality of life' difference."

I would think many women at that time would have been afraid to do that, because just getting the job, breaking in, is tough enough,

I said. What made you think you could get away with that? "Well, in retrospect, by the time I was at Bache I was lucky," Muriel answered. "I was doing well because accounting was vital in the industries I was covering—they played to my strengths. If I would have gotten food or utilities or something, I would have been nothing."

I asked Muriel to tell me about her leaving research in favor of trading. It turned out to be a long, complex process. "There was a man by the name of Walter Guttman at Shields & Company, a market analyst who wrote this crazy market letter with a tremendous following. He wanted to start his own firm and he said, 'I'm going to leave, do you want to come in as a partner?' And I said, 'Sure, I'll come in as a partner. Why not?' But," Muriel continued, shaking her head, "the exchange wouldn't approve him. I was mad, because I was out in the cold. The partners at Shields had heard about it and they called me in and said, 'We understand you're going to be in that group.' I said yes, if it goes through. They said, 'We think you should leave after today, here's a check for two weeks.' "

Although this deal fell through, by now Muriel was established on the Street. After a year and a half, she landed at another number firm, Finkle & Company, where she became a partner and her brokerage career continued to blossom. "I remember I got an opening order, a courtesy order, from somebody, and I went to the head of the company, Mr. Finkle, and I showed him this 5,000 share order and said, 'Isn't this great?' He looked at me and said, 'That's shit.' " Muriel let out a long laugh. "I'll never forget that! That's one of those things that stays in your head." Muriel waited a minute before continuing. "But it was a big deal for me. I mean, I used to be content just getting orders for the research that I was doing. I remember the first block of stock I ever did when Dan Finkle was trying to buy a railroad by the name of Gulf Mobile & Ohio. I found and placed the block and thought, 'I just made $5,000 doing this—this is wonderful!' "

As her career took off, Muriel also began to learn about some of the unwritten rules that dictate life on the Street, and the extent of her success really sank in. "Once I crossed some Beech Aircraft stock. It was only a small block. I was late, and the person I was meeting for lunch said, 'Where were you?' I said, 'I just came off the floor. You know, there's something wrong. I crossed a little block of Beech Aircraft and I made more today than my dad made as a dentist all year.' And he looked at me and said, 'You shouldn't even think that way. But if you do think that way, you should never talk about it.'"

It's funny, I said, because I've felt the same having made more a year than my father made in a lot of years. You feel a little guilty at first, but then you think, well, that's what it's all about. Muriel nodded in agreement. "That's what it's about—you're lucky you do this, you found a job where you're talented—but at the same time you just can't say, 'I'm entitled, Lord.' After I made x dollars, I realized that it's not the money that makes the difference. After you get to the point where you've got money, security, you realize it's a commodity—a very important commodity, but still just a commodity. And a lot of people don't understand that. They'll buy a house on the ocean in South Hampton . . ." Muriel's voice trailed off, and she shook her head.

. . . rather than give back a little bit to what gave them the money in the first place, I said.

"Yes," she said, pointing with her fork to underscore the point. "Give back some to the system."

Our breakfasts, late in arriving, were placed before us, and we ate for a moment in silence. Muriel had gotten ahead of herself. I wanted her to back up and tell me about an event that was a milestone for women in finance: when she became the first woman to get a seat on the New York Stock Exchange in 1967.

It wasn't a smooth process. She had a tremendous following and was doing an exceptional amount of business at this point in her career, handling all the biggest accounts, for example, placing 30 to 40 percent of the stock of Boeing in the institutions. The time seemed ripe. She initially got the idea from a client, Jerry Tsai, who thought she would never make partner in a large firm because she was a woman and would be better off just getting a seat and going into business for herself. Muriel was now approaching hurdles no one else had ever attempted to leap.

She was in a Catch-22 situation, however. The exchange, in an unprecedented move, refused to approve her seat until she had loan approval from a bank. The banks, in turn, refused to approve her loan until her seat was guaranteed by the exchange. It was her business savvy—and honesty—that made the difference.

"I had been on the board of a small company with a man who was the head of National Cash Register [NCR] and who was also on the board of Citibank. I was looking at National Cash Register and I kept saying, 'This looks cheap.' One day he said, 'Mickie, I think you're right, go to National Cash Register.' And I was right, you know, because the numbers on the depreciation indicated their earnings were going to balloon for a few years. I had large buy orders from institutions. One day someone at Chase Bank called and said, 'We just voted to sell our [NCR] stock, come on in for your bid.' I said, 'You shouldn't do that,' but he said, 'Hey, don't tell me, we already voted to sell it.'

"I had been doing a great deal of business with Chase. So I called a man I never knew, a Mr. Bridgewood, who was head of the trust department. I said, 'Mr. Bridgewood, I'm told I should come in with a bid, that I can have your stock. I'll take your stock at the market, but I don't think you should sell it.' He asked me why, and I told him. When I was done, he said, 'Thank you, that's very interesting,' and went back in there and canceled the sale, and he changed the vote on the committee so that not everybody else had an equal vote anymore. The guy that was running the Boeing fund that I used to do a lot of business with said, 'What is she? God?' and Bridgewood

said, 'No, she just knows more about the company than we do!' "
Muriel laughed.

"But that established another customer," she continued. "I
would call him and say, 'I think you should buy this because . . .' And
as it turned out, they were the bank that loaned me the money to
buy the seat when the other one wouldn't, so it was probably tied
into that.

"At that time, becoming a partner was possible only at small
firms: I had been a partner at Finkle, and I had been a partner at
Bremberg. The small firms—and this wasn't that long ago—were the
only place a woman could be a partner. There were no women partners at the major firms. But at the time, I still didn't think buying a
seat myself was a viable option. I said to Jerry, 'Don't be ridiculous,'
and he said, 'Well. I don't think there's a law against it.' But it still
wasn't easy. People like things status quo. I mean, when I think of
some of the nonsense . . ." Muriel rolled her eyes. "But that doesn't
exist today. Women can go in there and do what they want to do today, I think."

Because many of the women I've talked to say they feel they
have to work much harder than men, I found this comment rather
surprising, and I pressed her on this point. "If you have the money to
buy a seat, yes. But, that doesn't mean people will do business with
you. I think you have to prove yourself. Whether you have to prove
yourself more as a woman than a new man coming on the floor, I
don't know. As far as having to work twice as hard, well, that's true
in everything. *Fortune* magazine just did a story saying that women
are still working harder than men."

But I guess the difference, I said, is that on Wall Street, the rewards can be so much greater. "That's true—the money's there,"
Muriel observed. "I feel good about it, because a lot of women are
starting money management firms. And there, your end customer
doesn't care what you are—black or white or pink or yellow. All they
know is, if you outperform the Dow year after year after year, you're

making them money. But while money may be the great equalizer in some things, you don't see women in the executive suites. I think women are being paid pretty good money, but I'm surprised by a few of them who, after amassing a few million dollars, haven't started their own firms."

I asked her if she sees that changing soon. For a moment we talked about women we know in influential positions. While inroads have been made, it's apparent they are still the exception rather than the rule. Muriel has her own ideas, relating to how men and women interpret money and power, about why this is the case. What I find interesting and encouraging about Wall Street, I told Muriel, is that a lot of women don't necessarily equate money and power, but men do.

"Yes, men do—it's automatic. I used that in a speech I gave to a women's group recently. Money and power. I said that a lot of things won't change as long as the men have the money and the power, until women know how to use money and power. We don't even know how to use the fact that we start and own more than a third of all the new businesses. We don't use the leverage. When you employ people, that's power."

Muriel, I knew, had been involved in politics, first as superintendent of banks for New York State, then in an unsuccessful senate run in 1982. Did these issues, I asked her, have anything to do with your leaving the Street briefly and going into politics? "No, frankly, because I was offered that job, I wasn't looking for it. I got a call from [New York] Governor Hugh Carey." I had to laugh. This woman never seemed to have to fear for employment. Were you ever looking for a job? I asked. It seems like you're always at the right place at the right time.

"No, no," she answered, "there was one time between Bache and Shields where I sent a resume out under my name and I did not get *one* response—at first. Then I sent my resume out through the

New York Society of Securities Analysts with just my initials, and I got an interview and a job."

Muriel hesitated for a moment. "That was *part* of why I almost ran again for office. By the time I became superintendent of banks, I had enough money to live my standard of life. I got a call and Governor Carey said, 'I'm looking for a woman, and yours is the only name that keeps coming back.' I had never worked for him, I had never given him a dime. That was when I realized the power that government has in people's lives. And I said to myself, 'Gee, I could do better than some of these people in the Senate.' " I didn't win, but I asked for the nomination again in '87—I offered to put up a million bucks if I didn't have a primary. Because in the Republican primary, I'd get killed because I'm pro-choice. But without a primary, I wouldn't have gotten bloodied. In the primary, if you're a Republican, the Archie Bunkers come out, and if you're a Democrat, the crazies on the left come out. The extremes in both parties come out in a primary, not the middle-of-the-road people."

We turned the conversation back around to the Street. Muriel, rather than becoming a money manager, founded the brokerage firm that bears her name. Weren't you one of the first discount brokers? I asked. "Not in retail, but discount in general," Muriel answered. "I was on the front page of the *Wall Street Journal,* May 2, 1975. I knew the brokerage business, and I realized that research was not going to be paid for anymore, and that ERISA and the advent of negotiated rates were coming together. If one law had come in and not the other, it would have been a nonevent."

"At the time, we called ERISA 'Everything Ridiculous Invented Since Adam,' " Muriel laughed. "It said that the institutions had to get the best execution at the lowest cost, and at the same time we had the advent of negotiated rates coming in. If negotiated rates had come in without ERISA, the institutions would have continued to pay me for doing their work."

You strike me as such an exceptional person with people, I told Muriel: You have such charisma, you know how to talk to people, how to communicate with people, and I'm sure that's a large part of your success. It's an exceptional trait, because Wall Street has changed considerably over the years. "I'm honest. I have a Midwestern honesty. I just wouldn't know how to lie," Muriel responded. She put down her coffee and waved her hand. "Oh, the ethics on Wall Street . . . It's an interesting thing, because when I first came to New York and drove around in a little beat-up Studebaker, I used to see a Mercedes going by and I thought, if I work hard, I'll have one of those. If you looked at the people who were on Wall Street then, you would go broke before you broke your word." She looked me in the eye and stressed every word: "*You would go broke.* You didn't have tape machines to monitor conversations and orders. When I came back from the superintendent's post, I found out I was about the only discount firm who didn't have a taping machine. That wasn't the case before. Your word was your bond, period. I never had an institution renege. And yet, in the retail business, we would have been totally broke if not for the taping machines, because some of those customers said they said 'sell' instead of 'buy,' during the crash of '87."

"It was a different time, a different set of ethics. It's a shame. Some of these people today, the specialists in the business, they would have gone broke back then. I remember I was at Finkle & Company during the 1962 market break and those guys were standing up—the Ford Foundation had lent some of them money because they felt they had to buy those blocks—they had to make the market work. That's the way it was done, you just didn't think of anything else. Today, with some of these little punks with the derivatives . . . oh please!"

Muriel expressed more than a little exasperation at the huge speculators and derivatives jugglers who make headlines with increasing frequency, obviously considering them one of the less desirable elements of the new Street. What do you see ahead, I asked, given the way Wall Street's changed? Obviously, there's good and bad. "There are *some* positive things." She paused. "What do I see? I think it's going to take a couple more slaughters in the bond market with some arbitrage deals until you have wide margin requirements. There are no margin requirements on world currencies and most derivatives, for example. We need worldwide margins. You can't do it unilaterally in one country. I think there is a purpose in capital markets, and that's to raise money to help an economy. In the process of doing that there are places where smart individuals can make a lot of money. If you didn't have the capital raising mechanism, could you have had a Microsoft? A Netscape? An Intel? Or any of these great companies that are the new generation? The answer is *no.* It takes a very efficient capital market raising system to do it.

"So what are these guys doing?" she asked, referring to the huge speculators. "We have created a wonderful, global capital raising vehicle, and they're just taking their little piece out of it for themselves. I don't see them creating any economic value. I'll take my hat off to them, they're smart as whips, but what are they doing for the system?"

Do you see it coming to a critical mass? I asked Muriel. There are those who think the system is becoming almost too complicated in some ways. "Firms are taking more and more risk on in their trading," she answered somewhat ominously. "I think that derivatives have put an additional element of risk in there that we can't define. When I look at some of the highly leveraged positions that the people are taking—the hocking of treasuries at 97 percent, 98 percent margin—what are they accomplishing? It's not a matter that the treasury needs them to issue the bonds, it's a matter that *they're* seeing an arbitrage opportunity in there. Are they adding to liquidity? Probably." Muriel added this last comment without any enthusiasm.

But futures are derivatives, I pointed out. "The plain vanilla ones are different," Muriel answered. "I'm not saying they're wrong, I'm just saying if you use derivatives as an investor, corporation, or institutional buyer, you have to have the same knowledge as Wall Street." I mentioned that a friend of mine calls the new derivatives "gene-spliced." "Yes," Muriel said, "You do oil that's trading somewhere against LIBOR that's doing this, against this that's doing this, against coconut oil somewhere else, and you say 'you have a perfect hedge' but the company doesn't know what it's doing. Please!"

I asked Muriel about the present and future of her business. At the time of our interview, Muriel was in the process of taking her company public by purchasing 97.5 percent of a soon-to-be-liquidated furniture store chain, giving herself publicly traded stock with which to fund future expansion without holding a public offering. She was rather put out by a recent *New York Times* article that, among other things, cast aspersions on her method of going public. According to Muriel, the article was replete with factual errors and innuendo, despite her repeated attempts to provide the reporter with accurate information. She addressed the *Times* criticisms with the spunk you'd expect of a woman who has defied odds for decades.

"Currently, our client base is twofold. We have about 80,000 retail accounts, and those are individuals. In the capital markets, we work a lot of orders on the floor for two or three cents a share. And then we get involved in the underwritings. The reason I'm doing this is very simple. I think we're going to have some kind of consolidation in the industry. You don't have a currency when you're private, so you can't say to someone, 'We'll pay you so much in stock, and so much out of earnings for the next five years.' This way, I have a currency to deal in. I'm just saying there could be opportunities I will be in a position to take advantage of. Now, what am I paying for that opportunity? I'm paying 2.5 percent, which is not that much. The shareholders of the company will own 25 percent at no cost. If you do an IPO, you have to come out with at least 20 percent of the company. I don't want to sell company stock to the public when the firm does not need the capital; I don't want to sell any of my personal stock. What happens if the market turns down dramatically, do I want somebody to pay for my stock and then find that it's down a third?

"I wouldn't like it! I don't need it. I could raise new money for the company. But what would I do? I'd have to sit there with a pile of cash that says, 'I've got to put it to work,' because we don't need it in the firm now. We're currently, I believe, the largest clearing account National Financial Services has, and they're owned by Fidelity—they do Fidelity's clearing and ours. We're the largest outside clearing account. I've got a very good rate structure there. I could save a little money the other way, but we've got a good deal going now. Back-office work doesn't appeal to me."

Fair enough. I switched gears. Muriel gives a great deal of her time and money to women's groups and other charitable causes. Simply, she gives back. Because as a female-owned brokerage she has benefited from laws requiring minority participation in certain underwriting deals, she arranges to give commissions from these deals to charities selected by the parties to the transaction. To hear her say it, she couldn't live with herself if she didn't. She told me how it all started.

"On my birthday in 1990, I went to an awards ceremony for a man named John Torres. The story was, he was an ex-convict who convinced the street gangs to stop fighting when he was released. He started a place called Miracle Cadets. They're still in existence— Third Avenue and 106th Street—he works with single-parent kids. I found out he's saved hundreds of children, and he lives on eight or nine thousand dollars a year. I was sitting next to Robin Farkas and I said, 'So, you must be buying bonds in next week's city deal. We were just put into the syndicate. Give me your order, and I'll give the profit to this group.' That's how it started. I've benefited from some of these developments in the business. My firm has been placed in one underwriting along with two black firms, in the top bracket with Bear Stearns, Smith Barney—the big boys. Our revenues were over $400,000, and we donated half that. Am I supposed to take that $225,000 in commissions and put it in my pocket? This works out for everyone."

And you're giving back again, I noted. "But isn't that fun?" Muriel asked almost giddily. "Am I supposed to take that money, put it in my pocket and say, thank you, I'm entitled?"

A lot of people would, I couldn't help but say. "I couldn't fight the way I fight if I did that. I don't need it anymore. Now, I don't like to fight," Muriel smiled, "but if there's a big fight that I believe in, it's fun—if I fight for something bigger than myself. If it were a matter of fighting just to put something in my pocket, I couldn't do it. It would take on a sleaze factor. It wouldn't be right. If I make a point—that a woman-owned firm can perform on that level—then it's a good fight."

And like that, our morning was over. Muriel had an appointment to make, and I had to head back to the studio. The sun was still shining, so I took a short walk before catching another cab. I had a great deal of material to sift through, I thought. But I was left with one lingering impression. Whatever happens with Muriel Siebert & Company in the days and years to come, I know the woman at the helm will continue to fight the good fight.

Gail M. Dudack

Managing Director and Chief Investment Strategist,
UBS Securities, LLC

Imagine for a moment that you're a woman in a traditionally male-dominated business with few, if any, women in high-profile positions. Next, imagine that your peers have traditionally looked upon your work methodology as voodoo. Finally, picture yourself at the tender age of 25 appearing on national television as a mouthpiece for your industry.

That was precisely Gail Dudack's situation when she first appeared on Louis Rukeyser's *Wall $treet Week* 21 years ago as a young, female, technical analyst in a world full of older, male, fundamental analysts. She was, in effect, jumping three hurdles at once.

While she's become familiar to many market watchers over the years as a rotating panelist on *W$W,* as well as for her appearances on

CNBC and CNN, Gail has quietly built and maintained her reputation outside of the glare of the cameras through her meticulous research and analysis at such investment houses as the Pershing division of Donaldson, Lufkin, & Jenrette and SBC Warburg. Now chief investment strategist for UBS Securities, a leading international investment bank, Gail occupies a position that is the envy of any Wall Street professional—man, woman, technician, or fundamentalist.

As she ushered me into her Park Avenue office and seated me at a table a few feet from her desk, a computer humming and chirping in the background, Gail's very modern, bright, chrome-and-glass suite appeared to be the ultimate reflection of what technical analysis is all about: space-age, technology-driven market analysis, about as accessible and understandable as particle physics.

But her warm, low-key demeanor belies the somewhat imposing decor of her office: Gail struck me as reflective, soft-spoken, and self-possessed. It's an interesting contrast to the bluster that many Wall Streeters sometimes seem to cultivate to draw attention to themselves. While some seasoned traders and analysts compare battle scars acquired over lifetimes of crawling up the ladder, Gail gives the impression that her career was almost an accident—a nice surprise that sort of fell into her lap.

Her calmness and composure, however, camouflage a hardworking personality that actually loves the pervasive competition of the Street—this is, I would find out later, a woman who used to exchange punches with the high school quarterback. This interesting blend of quiet toughness and stability have made Gail Dudack one of the Street's top analysts and strategists, counseling institutional clients around the globe, as well as a presence among her peers. She was a founding member of the International Federation of Technical Analysts and is a former president of the Market Technicians Association, the two dominant (and overwhelmingly male) professional societies for technical analysts. She later served as a board member of the New York Society of Security Analysts and is currently a trustee of the Securities Industry Association Institute.

After we settled into our chairs, we exchanged some tips on combating spring allergies (mine had kicked in, and I was looking for a decongestant that didn't make me want to fall asleep in the middle of a broadcast) and talked a little about Wall Street in general. Many outsiders view the Street as a sterile, conservative environment. My experience, and the experience of people I know in the business, is that it's one of the most dynamic and exciting places to work in the world; the most adventurous souls say they were drawn to it in much the same way many people (including me) were drawn to journalism and broadcasting. Gail was no exception.

"Like anything, it was as much accident as design. I had an economics degree from Skidmore College, and I started to think about what I did *not* want to do. I did not want to be an economist, per se, I did not want to teach, and I did not want to work for a commercial bank. The one thing I knew was that I didn't want to have a job where I came in every day and knew exactly what I was going to do. I didn't know much about Wall Street, really. My parents had not invested in stocks and bonds, other than maybe local companies. But I thought it sounded really interesting, and the thing that I liked is that it seemed that Wall Street changed every day—that appealed to me. So, I actually tried Wall Street out when I was still in college as a summer job."

I was curious about how someone "tries out Wall Street." Most of the women I interviewed started their careers inauspiciously; they had to show the ability to put up with grunt work, taking any job they could get just to get their foot in the door. When I asked her what kind of job it was and how she landed it, she laughed. "It was in the research department at Pershing & Company," Gail remembered. "I just called up this New York number and told the operator I was looking for a summer job. She connected me to the research department at Pershing, and I was lucky to talk to the fellow who was second in charge of research at the time."

"It was my first experience, and I did everything. My main role was to substitute for every secretary who had a summer vacation, so I started out doing a lot of typing. I also worked with the librarian and went with different analysts to interview companies, listen to company meetings, and I got to work on spreadsheets, so I got a very broad-based view of research that summer. I took all the grief they threw at me as well: I think that came with the territory, considering I was doing this in the early '70s. I really enjoyed it, and I think it showed." Gail smiled and summed up the experience. "They eventually called me back for a permanent job, so obviously I typed well, or something," she laughed.

"I started out as a junior analyst, and in those days, before high tech, we had what was called the 'information center.' It handled the questions coming in from all the brokers in the network—and it was a large network, about 7,000 brokers at the time. That was the basic training program. You'd take those questions and either research them at the library or take them to the appropriate analyst to get them answered."

Even today, I noted, the Street is somewhat skeptical of technical analysis; back then it must have been even worse, especially for a woman—they'd have two reasons to doubt your qualifications. I wondered how and why Gail got involved in it.

"I was taking night classes in a variety of things, and I stumbled across technical analysis, although in retrospect I had stumbled on it before. When I went back to college my senior year I did two independent studies, one was on short interest, and one was on the 'odd-lotter,' who at that time was actually a phenomenon on Wall Street, and those turned out to be two technical studies. Many years later, I found those reports, and I said, 'Well, look at this.' I was interested in technical analysis before I had any idea what it meant."

I said it must have been fate and Gail nodded in agreement. "And I think at this point in my life I have a better understanding why," she said. "When we get to know ourselves, we can see how we function. I function as a visual person, not an auditory person, so when I look at data I have to picture it, I like to graph it. I took accounting—I know I can do it, but I hate it. Put some data on a chart, though, and I can interpret it quickly."

But what kind of insight does it give you that you wouldn't get with a more traditional fundamental approach? I asked.

Gail walked over to her desk for a second to punch up a quick chart on her computer, pointing to the screen as if it explained everything. "When you look at technical analysis, it's supply and demand, but it really focuses on psychology as well—it's the only area of stock market research or analysis that deals with that," she said. "While all these economic elements and fundamentals are underlying the market, the next 10 percent move in the market—at any moment in time—is going to be driven by psychology. It's how people feel. In retrospect, it was a natural for me, but I didn't know what I was doing at the time. Today, as a strategist, I analyze mostly fundamental and economic data, but again, I chart most of my models and try to relay my story to clients through a series of pictures or graphs."

At this point in her career, Gail was still one of many junior analysts in an anonymous research group. I pressed her on how she parlayed that into a position as a noted technician. "While I was taking these night courses, the technical analyst in our office quit one day, so I went into my boss's office and asked for the job. He didn't say 'no,' he said, 'Well, first you have to replace yourself.' At the time, the research area was getting computerized, so I wrote a manual on how to run the research center and how to run a database of information on all these companies that we followed and interviewed people to take over for me.

"At the same time, I volunteered to maintain all the company's charts at night, and I started writing reports about the market every day, which at this point just went straight to my boss, so he could see what I was doing. It took me six months to make the transition, and then another six months where I was undercover—I didn't really publish for clients, I just did some individual stock analysis and looked at the market and wrote sample market analysis/forecasts in a self-guided training program for a year.

"In some ways it kind of surprised me—I was pretty young, and I was writing about these things. I thought, 'Wow, I thought you had to be 50 before you could publish.' "

Listening to all this confirmed for me that Gail possessed one of the common traits of successful women on the Street: They take the initiative, assume extra responsibilities, and make the most of the situation they're in. They have in common the knack for turning sow's ears jobs into silk-purse careers. Gail was silent for a moment and shifted in her chair; she looked out the window, appearing to rethink her early career. When she spoke, it was as if something obvious had just dawned on her for the first time.

"You know, if I look back on some of the secrets of my success, it was that I was so naive—I'd just ask the switchboard operator about a summer job, or walk into my boss's office and ask for this technician's job." This comment seemed genuinely sincere—it didn't appear to be false modesty, even though it seemed to simplify the situation somewhat. Well, I pointed out, maybe you weren't naive, maybe you just knew what you wanted.

"I think I've always kind of known myself," Gail said, seeming to agree with my hypothesis. "I've counseled people trying to get into the business, and I think many times people don't really check themselves to see what they really like, what they're really good at, what they want to do. They just make an arbitrary decision, or are maybe pushed into it by someone else, or they're just going for the money—which was never really my motivation."

"In fact, when I went to work, I always felt I was going to end up with four children, a white picket fence—the housewife role. I never really intended to have a career. I'm part of that transition group where women didn't really yet participate in the workforce, they had families. That was something I expected to do and really always wanted. I'm lucky that I do have a family now."

The family versus career conundrum has brought down many a family and many a career—sometimes both. Gail has a husband and seven-year-old son. When I asked her if it was difficult to combine these elements of her life, she leaned forward and raised her voice a notch to get her point across.

"That's probably the most challenging thing, and the most wonderful thing. Without any doubt, having a family and having children, puts your entire life in perspective. It changes all of your priorities, as it should. But it adds such a wonderful balance. It makes most individual days challenging and difficult, but it adds so much to your life in the big picture—it's more important to keep focused on the big picture. I also have a wonderful husband. He's very supportive, very helpful, and we really share a lot of the duties. And our goals are the same, which is important."

Many women have a much tougher time making both work, and Gail's self-knowledge may have helped her resolve certain issues earlier on in life. Some people end up working their whole lives without doing what they want to do, I noted. Even though she didn't initially think she'd even have a career, Gail seemed to enjoy hers once she was in it.

"I loved it," Gail confessed. "When I started doing the technical work, I really did find a groove. When people ask, 'How did you do it?' I say, 'I think I looked at a million charts,' and it's probably not much of an exaggeration. In those first five or six years that's really what I did. I looked at stocks mostly and then started doing market letters. . . . I really stumbled into it."

When you started on the Street in research, I asked, were there many other women? "There were very few women," Gail said. "My particular department had two or three other women analysts, and Bernadette Murphy worked down the hall—I met her in the ladies' room. She is a few years older than me, is an amazing and wonderful person. She remains in many ways my role model and, I'm happy to say, a dear friend. So I did have, in my immediate area, a number of women."

While it shouldn't be surprising that the small circle of female Wall Street professionals at the time would bump into each other, her situation seemed unusual, at least judging from the other women I'd interviewed so far. They typically described being the only woman in their department or one of only two or three in the whole company. That must have been kind of nice, I told Gail.

"I think it was nice, although I never really thought of it. I didn't have trouble working with men. I think men had problems working with me, but I didn't have trouble with them."

That was an interesting way of putting it, I thought. I wondered if Gail was unconscious of, or perhaps impervious to, sexual discrimination on the street. Did men resent you, I asked her, or think you didn't belong.

"Well," she said, almost shrugging apologetically, "I found out much later that things like that were taking place, but again, I was extremely naive to it all. I remember one time there was an officer's dinner, and I was standing around with a bunch of traders. We'd all had quite a few glasses of wine, and one of them turned to me and said, 'You know Gail, we always thought you were a joke, but you really proved us wrong.' He hugged me and everything—it was meant very affectionately, and it came out only because there were a few drinks that had preceded it. But, it was a bit shocking to me because I was oblivious to it."

I wondered how I would feel if someone I used to work with revealed that he had thought I was a "joke." I can't imagine I would just shrug it off immediately. Did it change the way you felt about your job or did your job? I asked.

"Would it have affected me when I was younger?" Gail mused. "Perhaps. But at that point—especially because it was meant so well—no. I think it was because I always felt comfortable with men. When I was a teenager I was something of a tomboy and was always involved in sports and could talk the language." Gail mentioned a book she had seen years ago, a guide for women in business, that pointed out the differences between men's language and women's language, and how women who couldn't adapt to the male style were left out in the cold. This, she assured me, was not the case with her.

"I think those things put off a lot of women back then, but it didn't bother me. There were a number of times when people would come up and say something quite [she hesitated for a moment, smiling, to find the right word] . . . blue, right to my face to watch me blush, and I would give them a bunch of four-letter words right back and start laughing—that's when I became one of the guys. In high school, I was *always* one of the guys. In class I sat between the quarterback and the receiver of our football team—I was a cheerleader—and we used to punch each other in the gut in the locker room to see whose stomach muscles were harder. So I enjoyed that kind of stuff, and the language didn't bother me."

I thought it might be worthwhile to get Gail's take on the other side of the gender coin: possible advantages of being a woman on the Street. Other women had said they found it was an advantage; one noted that when she called someone they were perhaps a bit taken aback because she was a woman, but they were also a little more willing to talk to her because she was very pleasant, which helped her. I asked Gail if she thought it aided her in a similar way.

"I think it definitely did. The thing that's great about what I do is that you try to forecast the market, which is a ridiculous job when you think about it. You do, however, get a report card every day: You're right or wrong, so when you're right, you'll get acknowledged, and you'll probably be remembered more easily because being a woman is more unusual. Actually, if you look at Wall Street today and just list all of the strategists, there are quite a few women, which is really amazing. I remember when I joined the Market Technicians Association, I think there were about 100 members and only six of them were women, and I was the only one who worked for a sizable firm."

Apart from Bernadette Murphy, I asked Gail if there was anyone else who was a real influence or inspiration or who caused a turning point in her career. "It was a combination of people. The biggest turning point was probably when I met Louis Rukeyser, obviously. Reginald Oliver, who hired me for my summer job at Pershing, was also instrumental in putting together client seminars where Lou and I were both speakers, and he made sure that we met. That was how I got an invitation to be on *Wall $treet Week*—which I didn't think was real at first." She laughed a little remembering her reaction to the offer. "I thought it was like, 'We just built a pool, come on over for a swim sometime,' and I said, 'Oh, why thank you.' But it turned out to be a real invitation.

"There's a perfect example of where being a woman, I think, was a big asset. The show at that time was 7 panelists, and they were looking to expand it to 20. Lou, I think, has always been very forward-looking in putting together his show, and he was looking to add more women or other minorities. I told the producer, 'I know why you really want me: I fit three minorities: I'm a woman, I'm young, and I'm a technical analyst.' In those days, I was very unusual."

Women seem to be split on the benefits of media exposure, I told Gail. Some think it helps, others say it doesn't make a difference. Did it provide a boost? "I'm sure you're aware the media is quite powerful," she answered, smiling. "It's one thing to write a report, be right on the market, and distribute it to clients and to get that recognition, but it's another thing to be on international television. It has a completely different impact, even though it may seem subtle. It didn't really impact me or my job, or perhaps even my salary in the short run, but I think that exposure is definitely a big plus."

On the subject of salaries, I mentioned that another woman I'd spoken to said she moved from job to job very quickly because she was incensed that her male counterparts were getting paid twice what she was. Gail had some fascinating things to say about this subject.

"It's interesting. I feel that throughout most of my career I've been underpaid, but I didn't have a lot of resentment about it, because to me it was a security thing as well. I knew I was underpaid, I knew I was valuable. I hoped my employer knew it as well, but that's part of me—I've always wanted my employer to feel they're getting a lot more than their money's worth. And as a result, I've never feared for a job. There are trade-offs in absolutely everything, and that has been, perhaps, a conscious trade-off. It's a funny kind of thing: It's nice to be in the business all these years and feel mellow about it. Also, I think all things come in time, too—it's what you want at the time."

I would be surprised if most men would share your attitude, I said. They seem to naturally correlate money and power. Some of the women I've talked to said they had to push for salaries, but it sounds like you're telling me that's not the case, I told her.

"Perhaps because the job that I have, which is really providing research to clients, means that I am really a business. I'm not in the management track, and I think power is really meaningful only if you are in that track. I really feel I'm a mini–service industry unto myself. I remember one conversation I had with my first boss, Reginald Oliver, and I said, 'Thanks for being such a good boss,' and he said, 'Gail, you've never *had* a boss.' I was able to just do my thing. Power was never really a goal of mine. Being good at what I did was my goal."

With that in mind, I asked, has your career progressed the way you wanted it to do? Are you in the area you want to be in? "I'm glad to say, to a great extent, yes. A great deal came to me very quickly. I was on *Wall $treet Week* when I was 25 years old—I was a real baby. Then it slowed down and leveled off, and one day I just realized, 'Gosh, I'm really doing what I want to be doing.' Like anything in life, you've got to set goals. I constantly set goals for myself, things I wanted to accomplish, which is part of what makes life exciting. My goals keep changing, and I keep working at them until I achieve them."

Despite her calm exterior, I wondered if Gail was susceptible to the debilitating stress that can accompany a career on the Street, especially for women inclined to put in longer hours to keep up or get ahead. I mentioned that in my business there's also a lot of stress—a different kind of stress—that some people use to try to counter with drinking and drugs. I asked Gail if she noticed anything similar on Wall Street.

"When I started on Wall Street there was a lot of drinking. You would go out for a client lunch, and it would be very difficult to have three drinks and then meet other people after work and have drinks, drinks, drinks. But that's changed. It's mineral water now. Wall Street's gotten a bit more refined these days, I think."

Gail was also on the vanguard of another revolution that was beginning to sweep the Street at the time she entered the business: technology. Because it has been so instrumental to the increased application of stock analysis, in particular, I asked her what kind of impact she thought it had on the Street and her career.

"What computers have done for my work is to take a lot of the tediousness out of it. I would say 25 years ago, analysis was actually different, whether you were technical or fundamental. When I started, the hardest thing was to get the data. Really good analysts worked very hard at just *getting* information. Today, there's so much data available—everybody has it, everybody has a computer, everybody has the latest software—it's changed analysis. You can get to the point where you have so much data you might as well have *no* data, because you've got all of these things that are going to point you in different directions. There tends to be a great deal of confusion.

"So the question is, what should you be looking at today? What can put things in that big picture environment? It may not be what was important last week or last year. I view my work a bit differently now. I used to be more of a detective, finding data, collecting it, putting it together. Now, I'm checking out the data and trying to figure out what's relevant."

But I would think your experience from those early years would serve you well, because you know how to sift things out, I said. I don't think there's anything that can replace experience. I feel the same pressures you do about the speed of information, because there's so much coming at you, and a lot of people—and a lot of analysts, I'm sure—feel compelled to use it just because it's there. Gail looked me in the eye, smiled, and said, "Because you're asked to comment on it." (I laughed, because the people doing the asking are people like me.)

She continued. "And that's what's happened because of advances in communications, technology, computers, and data; There's a tremendous amount of instant analysis being done, which by its very definition can't be good analysis. Sometimes you get caught—and I have been asked many times to give an instant interpretation—but I won't let myself get trapped by something I said. Or, sometimes I probably frustrate you guys because I won't comment at all. Many times I get a call and someone asks, 'What happened today?' and I'll say, 'Well, nothing.'"

That's very savvy, I told her, because a lot of people seek out that limelight. You know, we have to sort through people—without naming names—that are always ready to comment on anything, and to a certain extent, that dilutes their value to the media. If you're a "tougher get," it almost makes you more valuable.

"I'll talk to you," Gail conceded, "but I'll try to tell you the truth, which may be 'today's market doesn't make any sense.' That doesn't make for good copy, but it happens. I think I try to be extremely honest in all my work, and when I don't know, I don't know. Sometimes we get pressured in this business to have an opinion, and you can make mistakes that way."

What I've found interesting, I responded, is that many people have this image of Wall Street as a very staid, conservative place. My experience is that you constantly have to be keeping up and changing and coming up with new things. What advice, I asked Gail, would you have for women who are considering work on Wall Street? Do you think it's gotten better as you've gone along?

"I think it's gotten easier for women to get into this business. I think it would be good to test it out, like I did. Try it out, see if it fits. The one thing I say to all recent graduates—and they are all so intense and work so hard—is that your first job doesn't have to be your last job. Be willing to make a mistake. If you think you want Wall Street, get a job—doing anything. If it's being a clerk on a desk or a secretary in a research department, do that, see if you like the environment, the people, the pace, and if so, work at it. If not, try something else, because Wall Street's not for everyone. It draws a lot of people, like a magnet, because it's exciting and because there's money—which is true—but there's also an awful lot of work, and long hours.

"I really think that some of the best and brightest minds are drawn into our business, but it *is* the most competitive industry anywhere. And if you don't like that kind of environment, then Wall Street is not for you. There might be a niche you can find, but for salesmen, analysts, it's not somewhere you'll succeed if you don't love the competition."

What's fascinating is that you probably wouldn't, at first glance, peg this composed, well-spoken analyst as a fighter who would thrive on the kind of competition she described. But apparently she does—the proof is in the results. As we wound up our interview, Gail gave me a tip on some allergy pills she'd found that didn't put her to sleep. I thanked her as she walked me to the door and went out to find a drugstore. I had a battle of my own to fight—with my allergies. The search for a better decongestant, not unlike the search for the next hot IPO, never ends.

Grace Fey

Executive Vice President and Director,
Frontier Capital Management

My first impression after stepping into Grace Fey's office was that I'd taken a wrong turn somewhere and entered the National Geographic Hall of Fame. All the walls of her sunny, many-windowed office are adorned with African wildlife photographs: cheetahs, zebras, lions, antelopes. At first, this effect obscures the more personal touches that are no less prolific. Grace's husband, Ted, figures prominently on her desk, represented by no less than six pictures. There is also a big bouquet of flowers from a broker at Dean Witter, a coffee cup from Piper-Jeffrey, a Disney paperweight, and what I thought at first glance might be a *real* wildlife specimen, but turned out to be her "lucky bunny" (more on that later).

The view from Grace Fey's window is not a snapshot of the suit-and-tie bustle of Wall Street, nor any part of the Manhattan skyline, for that matter. To her east, she can see ships sailing in and out of a harbor—big, lumbering commercial freighters circled by various smaller cruisers and sailboats with brightly colored canvas billowing in the breeze. If she looks toward Charlestown, she has a bird's-eye view of the Bunker Hill Monument. It's a panoramic view, all right—of Boston. As I looked around and remarked that she must feel like she's sitting on top of the world, Grace spun around in her chair, surveyed the scene, and smiled broadly. "Yes I do!" she said. "Seven windows, nineteenth floor, downtown Boston—I've come a long way."

She has indeed. As executive vice president and director of Frontier Capital Management Company, Fey personally manages over $320 million in assets for the $2 billion–plus investment management firm.

Perhaps it's just the unique New England setting, but Grace Fey is an interesting contrast to the sometimes frantic pace of Wall Street's money managers. Trim, athletic, and attractive, she somehow manages to be simultaneously energetic and relaxed. Maybe everything seems a little slower paced when you're removed from the immediate vicinity of the Street. After a brief rundown of each of the animal photographs on her walls, and an explanation of where the flowers came from, we talked a little about how she got her start, and why she's in Boston instead of Wall Street. Early on, it seems, she made an important friend and business associate—a relationship that so far has spanned her career.

"I began working in 1970 at Alliance Capital Management. My first boss was Don August, an analyst and vice president at the time. The funny thing is, today Don and I are partners at Frontier Capital," Grace smiled. "Don was very responsible for my getting into this business at all. I hadn't the slightest intention of being an analyst when I graduated from the University of Maryland. But as Donald's assistant, I fell in love with the business, and he really pushed me to go on."

Although they both subsequently went on to different jobs, the pair still maintained contact. "We stayed in touch over the years," Grace remembered, "even though he went to Putnam and then on to found Frontier in 1980. I went off to Keystone Investment Management Co. and then to Winchester Capital Management. I worked with private clients and Don worked with institutions, but we still remained good friends. Then in 1988, Frontier wanted to start a private client business and Don asked me to get involved. I said sure, but I'd like to stay in Boston."

When I asked Grace if there were many women in the business at that time, she shook her head and revealed how few role models she had. Whereas a male Harvard graduate might have been offered a promising finance position, women with comparable academic credentials found it more difficult to break into this exclusive club. Grace, like many others, initially took whatever job she could get and tried to work her way up. "No, there was only one woman that I knew of, an analyst at Alliance—Jane Mack," Grace recalled. "All the rest of us were secretaries, and we absolutely idolized her. Most of us were from Holyoke and Smith, and other top-of-the-line schools, but there just weren't opportunities then for women to manage money."

Grace, however, resolved to push ahead, and although it didn't happen overnight, she achieved an important goal in her career. "After five years at Alliance, I was determined to get my CFA (Chartered Financial Analyst) distinction. Alliance was only hiring Harvard Business School graduates at that time, so I left and started to work on my CFA at United Business Service, where I was hired as an analyst. After two and a half years there, I was hired by what is now Keystone Investment Management Company as a portfolio manager and analyst. I'd made it out of the traditional woman's position in the industry to professional status."

Grace now heads a group that specializes in individual investor portfolios and manages growth and balanced portfolios for private clients and smaller institutions. Like many women responsible for huge sums of money, her schedule requires a strict time management regimen—there's a great deal to accomplish each day. I asked her what her typical workday is like.

"A typical workday for me begins early with planning and organizing my daily schedule," Grace explained. "I always have a very full agenda. The first thing I do is check the previous day's performance to see how our products did relative to the market. I'm a morning person, so I try to take care of all communications with clients early. I also go through the mail and read any relevant material, and I read the papers every day—*Investors Business Daily* and the *Wall Street Journal*. I have lunch either with a client, management, or an analyst who is in town presenting an industry or stock. In the afternoon, I first tackle the 'headwork.' We have seven full-time analysts who do a lot of the legwork, and for the balance of the afternoon I talk with them and analyze the markets. I usually leave the office around 6:30 or 7:00, then go to the gym and work out with weights, and arrive home at about 8:00 P.M." She looked down at her desk for a moment and seemed to appreciate the demands of her schedule. "Every day's very full," she noted.

I've learned a little about the investment management business from the hundreds of interviews we've conducted on CNBC. The other interviews I'd conducted confirmed my impression that despite the presence of some gender barriers, women can excel on Wall Street because of the emphasis on the bottom line. I mentioned to Grace that if performance is there, it doesn't seem to matter whether an analyst or money manager is male or female; maybe that's why women are flocking to this business in greater numbers. "You're right," Grace agreed. "Competition is intense, but it's not a gender issue. Competition is just a fact of life in the investment management business as a whole. When it was in its infancy, there were fewer money managers, but it's always been intensely competitive. Before 1970, there were bank trust departments, but the investment management business really began with ERISA (Employment Income Securities Act) in 1974. In '73 and '74, pension funds lost 60 to 70 percent of their investments; that motivated the establishment of guidelines and the 'prudent man' rule. It also opened the door to hiring professional money managers, like myself. In 1980, there were 5,000 money managers; now in 1996, there are around 28,000. Decent performance becomes a given. You need to be in the top 50 percent of money managers to grow a business. Obviously, if you're in the top quarter on a consistent basis you grow a lot faster, and if you don't perform you fall by the wayside."

I asked Grace if she feels she got a "fair shake" in the industry. Appropriately, she thinks the put-up-or-shut-up performance standards of the Street help contribute to fairness between the sexes.

"Absolutely," she said, "because performance can be precisely measured every day. So many other positions in business are somewhat subjectively evaluated, but the investment management business is quite objective." However, she conceded that some difficulties do exist. "But this doesn't mean that there aren't any gender problems. I certainly had one situation in my career where my gender proved to be a handicap. I was a junior partner at a Boston-based investment management firm. I had been with the firm almost from its inception and had been on staff about six years. We had taken on a new partner who was rising in terms of control. I always had the best performance in the firm, I knew I was a main contributor, and I wanted to be given more stock—a larger piece of the equity. This particular fellow said to me, 'You know, for a woman you make a lot of money. If I were you, I'd go back to my office and be happy just to have the job.' And then he added, 'As a matter of fact, for a woman without a Harvard Business School degree, you *really* make a lot of money." That was the only blatant experience I've had of gender prejudice, and I've been in the business 26 years."

I could feel my blood pressure rising somewhat as she told me the story. When I asked her how she handled the episode, Grace explained that rather than letting it get to her, she used it as motivation to push on with her career. "That incident propelled me out of that firm and on to bigger and better things," she said. "Even though that was the only really negative experience I've personally run across, there are still definitely impediments to women in general. There are still people out there who will try to stand in a woman's way, but that's true of any profession. However, this business is very performance oriented; if a woman is really good, she can definitely make it despite the obstacles."

One challenge common to both men and women on the Street is adapting to the rapid and continuous change technological innovation has brought to the industry. Anybody working on the Street over the past 10 or 20 years has to be amazed by how dramatically technology has transformed the profession. Time frames that were once months, weeks, or days are now days, minutes, or seconds. Information, the real "product" that drives Wall Street, is distributed instantaneously. Volume on the Big Board often hits 500 million shares a day, and the number of mutual funds has skyrocketed—all of this driven by technology. Everyone has a PC at his or her desk and is networked in one way or another: We have the globe, and the global markets, at our fingertips. Analysts and traders are expected to absorb and interpret more information in less time than would have been thought possible only a relatively few years ago. Like many forms of technological progress, though, the promise of improved work or an eased workload comes at a price: Technology has actually intensified the competition and pressure of the business.

"Previously, if there was a major change in strategy, a salesperson would call us up by phone," Grace noted. "We might be the first or the hundredth call, depending on how much free business we'd brought to that institution—notification would arrive days or weeks later by mail. Now any change is instantaneously on the computer. Instantaneous information has added even more pressure and competitiveness to the business. It's often hard to get an edge. It also allows you, however, to manage more clients, have more efficient systems, and provide better service to clients."

Maybe the hectic pace is unavoidable on the Street or off it, after all. I know only too well from my own life that there often just doesn't seem to be enough time for business and personal life; given Grace's description of her average day, I wondered how she juggled career and family. She gave me a big smile and sighed, saying, "It ain't easy." We both laughed. The career/family problem has a limited number of solutions, and Grace seems to have opted for one that has become increasingly popular among working women, especially those realistic ones who have survived in the business trenches for a while and understand the compromises that come with the territory: She's cutting back—and has made some hard choices.

"I used to work 8 to 11 hours a day, and weekends, but I don't do that anymore. I still have to travel a lot; I'm out of town on average two days a week. I got married a little bit later than most women, at age 36. My husband, Ted, is a scientist and venture capitalist, so we both have really demanding careers. At first, we really wanted to have kids, but then reality set in. How could we possibly manage our lives? So we agreed not to. That definitely is an advantage from a career standpoint because I'm not pulled in a lot of different directions. Women today still end up being the primary caretakers of children, despite the changes in society. I watch some of my associates try to juggle children, marriage, and career. It's extremely difficult."

As it stands now, Grace seems to have managed a more than workable arrangement, within the limitations she's acknowledged. She's devoted to her work but still has a life and interests outside of it. "My husband and I live in Boston; it's a great city. I have a 15-minute walk to work and Ted takes the subway. When we leave work, we're home. We don't have to commute and we can spend all our free time together. We also have some extracurricular activities in the community. I'm on the University of Massachusetts Board of Trustees, and I'm also the chairman of our zoo." She pointed to the pictures on the walls. "Hence, all the animal pictures in my office. These activities are important to achieving balance in our lives."

After hundreds of interviews and spending countless hours with some of Wall Street's most successful professionals, I'm still interested in a person's particular recipe for success. Forging a successful career on Wall Street goes beyond knowing what stocks to buy or sell. Although to outsiders the end result may seem the same, each person has a unique experience and perspective, a singular approach that has made them what they are. When Grace shared her secret with me, I was struck by the value system she seems to share with other women on the Street: A concern for the personal touch and an appreciation for relationships that go beyond business and balance sheets. She is able to connect with people, understand their needs; and as result, her business flourishes even more.

"I think what makes me *feel* more successful than picking stocks or any of that, is my client relationships. For instance, I currently have two clients that I've had since 1978. Performance is important, and that's obviously what clients are hiring me for, but to be able to provide good results for a specific person, to meet actual needs, now that's hard to beat in terms of job satisfaction. With individual investors, I strive to understand their particular risk tolerance and what makes them happy. That also makes me happy and successful at what I do."

I asked Grace if her approach is different than her male counterparts. She swiveled in her chair and considered for a moment. "I think women have a different emphasis. For instance, I have one widow client who started with 60 percent of her investment in equities and 40 percent fixed income. By the end of the year, 1994, she was very upset. I took the time to really talk it out with her. Losing any money at all was absolutely terrifying to her. So I cut her back to 20 percent equities and 80 percent fixed income. She's now 67 and very happy. Any financial planner would objectively say she should have more in equities from a purely strategic standpoint, and I don't disagree with that. But you have to understand a person's individual makeup. A lot of men don't take the time to get to really know their customers. I think women do a better job of asking relevant personal questions."

It is this appreciation of the human variable that sets Grace apart. Such skills are easily described, but less easily acquired. And given the amount of money she handles and the profile of her typical client, the importance of people skills can't be underestimated.

"Our private clients are high net-worth individuals. For instance, my minimum in the private client sector is one million dollars, while the minimum on our institutional side is five million. I work with 'Mr. Entrepreneur,' while my partners work with company pension plans. I really listen to my clients and try to understand what their actual personal needs are; their needs are not often those described in a textbook. Communication, listening, and understanding are the keys. Usually, by the time a client sees me, he or she has already been screened by a consultant or financial planner, and I've been determined an appropriate match for that client. But over time a person's needs change. You have to keep listening to understand clients' current concerns, their family situations, what's actually going on in their lives. To me, helping someone personally is a better measure of success than picking a hot stock." Grace then smiled a big, broad smile. "Although I am happy that I was in technology last year, and I still have 25 percent of my portfolio in technology. I got a lot of pleasure out of picking Microsoft and Hewlett Packard, but even that was not quite as fulfilling as my client relationships."

The word "intuition" always seems to surface when I ask women on the Street if they perceive a difference between how men and women look at investing. Grace remarked, "Oh, definitely, there's a gender difference there. Women are definitely more intuitive. They interact with people differently; people can be much more open with a woman. I think women also bring a different perspective to the table. A woman may see things that somebody who's just crunching numbers may not. It's almost as if women have a more general, macro view. You definitely need both, though—I'm not saying you should fly by the seat of your pants, just sensing your way. Both aspects, logic/deduction and gut feeling/intuition, are important."

When I asked Grace what she thinks the future holds for women on the Street, she became very animated. Even taking into account any bias that may stem from her own exceptional level of success in the business, she's bullish on the prospects for other women in her industry, and forthright about the positive attributes women bring to the game.

"One day, women could easily outnumber men," she claimed. "We have 31 people total. We have four directors, three men and myself. But my whole division is made up of women. I didn't set out to do that—it's just a sign of the times. On the institutional side, we have one woman analyst and we're trying to get another because we think there should be a better balance. We're kind of like a family at Frontier—the chemistry within the firm as a whole is important. People contribute different, unique strengths. We feel it would be good balance to have another woman, and as we grow, hopefully we will have many more. It's not only good for the women, it's good for the business because of the different orientation they bring to the company."

So what would she tell a young woman just starting out? "It's a wonderful business!" Grace concluded. "It's very challenging, fulfilling, and creative. There are a lot of opportunities for women.

We've made great strides in the financial services and investment ends of the business, but there are still few senior level women in investment management. It would be great to see more women coming out of business school choosing the investment profession. There are a lot of women now in consulting—that's been a real big area, and a number of women in corporate finance and analysis, but it would be nice to see more women portfolio managers and women running their own firms. I would tell any young woman starting out to definitely get her MBA. I didn't, but undeniably, I was lucky," she said, sinking back into her leather chair.

I finally asked her about the lucky bunny.

"Well," said Grace hesitantly, "don't tell anyone, but when it's turned a certain way, it seems to coincide with the markets going up." She paused, and I waited to find out the answer.

"But I won't tell you which way," she said with a wink.

Maria Fiorini Ramirez

President and CEO,
Maria Fiorini Ramirez Capital, Inc.

It was the worst type of day to head into Manhattan—cold, rainy, and incredibly windy—but Maria Fiorini Ramirez is a very busy woman and I had to seize a rare interview opportunity. Around her office, almost right on the Hudson River at the World Financial Center, the wind was blowing so hard that I could barely make it to the revolving door. After negotiating an escalator and two crowded elevators, I finally arrived at Maria Fiorini Ramirez Incorporated.

Once inside I could tell it was a busy day in the markets: I could hear the frantic sound of shouting traders escaping from the other room. Maria met me in the lobby and led me through the crowded trading room packed with computers, trading machines, and TVs all tuned to CNBC so her staff could monitor the market and listen to interviews throughout the day.

Maria's office is adjacent to the trading room, but it feels like a million miles away. Her desk is piled with papers, plants, books, and a collection of baseball hats Maria swears she's going to mount on the wall some day. Shelves overflow with mementos from her years of globe-trotting: A beautiful Japanese fan is mounted on the wall, and next to that a picture of a hotel in Positano, Italy, that her friend runs. (She occasionally arranges reservations for some clients.) It's a relaxed, informal environment.

Maria is one of those genuinely warm, outgoing people who make you feel good about yourself—you want Maria to like you, because you like *her* so much. Given to laughter, and broad smiles, she immediately makes you feel at home.

She calls herself a "matchmaker," working hard to put people in touch with other friends or clients she thinks have something to offer each other. She has a seemingly endless supply of energy, knows everyone on the street, and has built a global advisory business in a matter of just a few years, working 25 hours a day. She considers every relationship a friendship rather than just a business arrangement, one of the distinguishing marks of her personality and a primary reason for her success. As an economic advisory and money management firm responsible for over $100 million, Maria Fiorini Ramirez Capital shapes investment decisions globally. Clients around the world look to her insightful analysis to keep abreast of market conditions and form trade strategy.

In a world where competition and attrition can sometimes put a strain on business and personal relationships, Maria has maintained and expanded a remarkably loyal following over the years. Born in Italy, she spent her early years in a small town on the slopes of Vesuvius, a volcano near Naples, and until recently she has retained her Italian citizenship, as well as a lovely Italian accent. Maria seems to bring a bit of old-fashioned, old-world charm and work ethic to her corner of the Street.

Her bicultural background has also played a significant role in her career, bringing her early exposure to international clients and an appreciation of the factors that move the global marketplace. A popular speaker around the world, Maria understands what makes both people and markets tick.

As I found out, Maria got started on Wall Street early, but her beginnings were anything but auspicious. She took a clerical job at Minehard Commercial (which was part of the C-I-T Group, and is now part of Dai-Ichi Kangyo Bank) after graduating from high school in 1967, but her positive outlook and work ethic steadily propelled her toward better things. I was surprised she was even interested in finance or the Street at that age. She certainly had few, if any, female role models to look to at the time.

"Well," she said quietly, "the reason I was so interested in finance was because when I was in high school I was studying for a very basic commercial degree. I hated typing, I hated stenography, so I thought, well, if I don't have steno then I can't be categorized as a secretary when I look for a job," Maria laughed. "Most of the better students were either going to medical school or something like that, and the other side of the coin for girls was to be a secretary when you got out of high school. You know, you get out and you work for Western Union or AT&T—that was like the dream job at that time.

"But because I didn't have the skills as a secretary, I could only get a job doing clerical work, and that's when I decided to go to night school. I went to Pace University because it was downtown and they had a very flexible program where you could go to school at night and on the weekends. And at the time economics was considered a boring, difficult subject, so I thought it would be a good challenge!" Maria laughed again. "I got the degree in about three and a half years and I worked for American Express."

What was it like being a woman on Wall Street at that time? "I think it was great," Maria said, "I think that because there weren't that many women around, you had to be a little tough-skinned, you had to ignore some things around you in order to move on and not let them bother you—water under the bridge."

When I asked her about any personal experience with prejudice or discrimination, Maria sounded some familiar themes I'd heard from other pioneering women: Yes, men were paid more or advanced more rapidly, but that's the way it was back then, and if you wanted to get anywhere, you just had to dig in and work harder.

"It's funny because I really didn't know what prejudice was." She considered again briefly. "Maybe there was some of it, but I didn't really let it bother me. I always thought if you got on with the job and got things done, people would appreciate you in the long run. There were always men around you that were at the same level who moved ahead faster or got paid more, but that was the normal thing to see then, so I always thought in the long run if you did better, stayed a little longer, worked a little harder, and learned a little more, you'd be better off—no matter what."

The key to Maria's "work ethic," I found out, is that she doesn't consider what she does work.

"I think if you like what you do, it's not work—and I really *love* what I do. Sometimes I can't believe that you can be as happy as I am doing what I'm doing and actually make a living at it. Most people, I think, look at their work as merely a job, but to me work is my life. Yes, I have other things in my life that make it very fulfilling, but I really look forward to getting up in the morning and doing this every day—and night, too."

Maria toyed with one of her baseball caps as she continued to describe her approach to work. "Sometimes I get up really early and call some clients in Europe when I know their day is just getting started, or you can be up late at night and call some clients in Asia to find out what's going on. I have always been very globally minded. The U.S., in terms of this business, has really been getting up to speed within the last five years, which makes it much more interesting."

Do you suppose you think more globally because you were born in Italy and spent your early years in Italy? I asked "Well, I think that if you've migrated it makes you a slightly different individual. If you're born in one country and then raised in some other place, you have another culture that is never really taken away from you. I think if you're raised biculturally you have a certain advantage. In my case, at least, I think it made me appreciate being here a lot more."

Your background didn't seem to portend a high-flying career on Wall Street, I noted. Was there a person in your life, in your family, or a friend who was a mentor or a real motivator for you to do what you do? "Well, nobody in my family did what I do, but my parents always stressed school, school, school—go to school, go to school!" Maria said, laughing. "I think that kept me working and going to school at night—doing it all—because I believed I could have a better life, a better job. When you're young you think of other things, but in the end I'm glad I did it the way I did. I got a good nuts-and-bolts background of business—and went to school and made my parents, and myself, very happy."

Maria then returned to her early days in the business. "Basically I was a clerk when I started in '67. I started in what was kind of a back-office position. I covered funds work, which was the area of the bank that handled travelers' checks and receivables and that kind of thing. It was the best education I could have gotten because it was an international bank: There were clients all over the world, and dealing with those clients and their needs made me very, very familiar with all the financial institutions outside the U.S. Later on, when somebody would mention the name of this or that institution, I would recognize the name, know who they were, and maybe have had some correspondence with them.

"I also did work on the credit side," Maria continued, seeming to remember, bit by bit, the myriad duties she attended to. "I learned how a balance sheet was structured, how to rip it apart, and how to make some sense out of it. It was a good way to learn the basics of banking. I worked in foreign exchange, I worked in payments and receiving, I worked in all the operational sides, so I really knew how the banking business worked, backwards and forwards. It made me aware of what kind of transactions were taking place and how they were finalized. This is all valuable information, because in this day and age its very difficult to instill in people the necessity of knowing how a business works from top to bottom. You can be armed with all kinds of degrees, but if you don't have some knowledge of the basic functions of the world that we live in, it's very hard to understand the more advanced concepts."

Having made the most of her experience at American Express, where she worked from 1968 to 1972, Maria felt it was time to move on. And although she was committed to her work and determined to make light of any discrimination, some inequities were evident during her tenure there and helped prompt her exit. "Well, I started to learn there's a difference between men and women in the business. At American Express when I was going through the program and wanted to know when and where I'd be going overseas, which I wanted to do, I was made aware that it would be highly unlikely because it was just not done.

"Some of my colleagues felt that maybe I should take some steps to change that, but it turned out to be a moot point, anyway. A friend and coworker of mine at that time was looking for a job, and one day we went to lunch with a headhunter—and I got a job. So, I basically left American Express because it was so easy to get

MARIA FIORINI RAMIREZ | *133*

another job. But it was the right thing to do because I was not working at the right place, where I could learn a lot and really enjoy what I was doing in the atmosphere that I was in. That's when I ended up going with an Italian bank, Banca Nazionale del Lovoro, for a year.

"I still thought that maybe I could go back to Italy at some point. You know, you always have this dream of going back to your homeland, but I soon realized that was not going to happen. Luckily, I had a friend at American Express who had moved over to Merrill Lynch. She told me they were looking for someone to build a credit department, so I interviewed and got the job. I was with Merrill Lynch for 10 years, and I loved just about every minute of it—it was a great place. But my early experiences were key. If I'd had easy surroundings, I never would have succeeded. . . . It was having to work hard and always be building from the ground up that has made me tough.

"I started out in the credit department, but shortly after that I started doing research in the trading room. It was a very exciting place to be, although there was a lot going on that I didn't understand—I didn't always understand the terminology. But I learned what was going on in the markets every day and that helped me keep our clients informed. I started a sort of news service or commentary, and it really caught on. Because I was talking to Merrill's clients worldwide everyday, I basically created my own international presence, and I eventually expanded to doing seminars all over the world for Merrill—Asia, Latin America. It was a lot of fun. And by doing that, I could meet the people I had been talking to over the years. I think that allowed me to really work on developing a personal relationship with clients."

It was fascinating to hear Maria speak so casually about going from a fairly anonymous banking job to an "international presence" in such a relatively short amount of time, as if it were the easiest thing in the world. But her gift for people, especially her skill at connecting with foreign clients, shined from the start.

"Building a network of relationships really takes a lot of work. I'm lucky, because I love different cultures: You learn so much about how different people view the world, how they view the market. It's invaluable knowledge, and because in essence I *am* a foreigner, I think I can relate to them better—I've had some of their difficulties, English as a second language, for instance—and as a result they're much more appreciative because they have someone who understands them. So I think I ended up spending more time than some of my colleagues with our foreign clients. And really, it takes so little to go out of your way to help people and try and understand them better—it really cements the relationship."

It sounds like the perfect place for you, I mentioned. Why did you leave if you were so happy? "I left not because I was unhappy, but more because I wanted to try something new again. It goes back to needing a challenge. I went to A. G. Becker Paribas—a number of my friends from Merrill had gone there—but when I got there I realized the place was not in very good shape: The first day I got there people started telling me that it was going to go out of business! And I thought, 'Oh no, it's not,' because I couldn't accept that I had made a mistake in going there."

She considered for a moment, and in true Maria form, managed to put a positive, personal spin on the situation. "But maybe it wasn't a mistake, because I made friends there I still have today. I also learned how people behave when they're under a lot of pressure and stress: The best and the worst comes out. It was the kind of situation that builds character. So, one day I'm there working as an economist, and a few days later the firm went out of business!" (Ironically, Becker was snatched up by Maria's previous employer, Merrill Lynch.)

"So," Maria continued, shrugging, "I moved on to Drexel, and some other people from Becker either went ahead of me or followed me. When I started there in 1984, it was still a small firm so you could really make your mark. In the time I was there, we went from being on the bottom of the list of primary dealers in the asset-backed business and treasuries to one of the top three. I worked in the high-grade fixed-income division, and it was a great experience."

As anyone in the business remembers, Drexel Burnham Lambert was one of the most conspicuous '80s success stories, an aggressive firm that went, as Maria recounted, from relative anonymity to the head of the class in a short space of years. Under the tutelage of Michael Milken, the firm became almost synonymous with the highly leveraged "junk bond" market, which, until its collapse in the early '90s, propelled the company. Drexel's fall, and Milken's, is well chronicled and sent shock waves up and down the Street. Were you there, I asked Maria, when Drexel was dissolved?

"Yes. I was kind of like 'till death do us part,' " she chuckled wryly. "There were many times I could have left the firm for a high-paying job elsewhere, but at the time most of us were just interested in surviving—in many areas of the Street times were hard—and every day it seemed like there was another article about Drexel: 'Was it going to survive?' But I decided I wanted to stay there and see it through, I wanted to be there for the challenge. I also felt very, very strongly that I needed to stay and help the friends I still had at Drexel through this tough time. If I left the firm at that time, I wouldn't have been able to sleep well."

Maria leaned forward in her chair. "It was *incredibly* draining. Plus, just being at Drexel you got accused of being part of things that you had absolutely no knowledge of. In a situation like that, just through association, people question your character. I remember talking to a reporter—this was somebody I'd known for many years—and he said, 'You must know what's going on there, you work there. You must be part of it.' You didn't really know who your friends were anymore.

"In fact, the day that Drexel went down, I was going to do a TV spot for CNBC. It was about 9:00 A.M. and just as I was about to go on there was a news item about Drexel dissolving. That's how I found out. I rushed back to the office and we all listened to the squawk box to hear what the firm was saying. By the end of the day, that was the end of Drexel. It made me incredibly sad."

Maria, however, was not a woman to be kept down for long. "I picked myself up and asked myself, 'Well, what do you want to do now?' But answering that question was harder than I thought. I didn't know exactly what I wanted to do, other than I knew I didn't want to go through that same anguish again with another firm—it was just too painful. It wasn't as bad for me as it may have been for some other people. Imagine being in your 50s and having worked somewhere for years, and suddenly you're out, but you still have the mortgage to pay, the college tuition to pay. . . . It's happening all over America with downsizing now. That's when I decided to start my own firm. I thought, 'I can do this on my own.' I had worked up a huge client list from my days of doing market commentary at Merrill, so I talked to everyone I could about starting up a business from scratch.

"Also, through my affiliation with Merrill, I got to know some people at John Hancock, and I called them to talk to them about becoming a subsidiary of them or developing a relationship with them. They wanted a global fund that was managed outside to eventually bring in-house, and I convinced them I could bring the best people on board. So I struck out on my own, but not entirely, because I had John Hancock behind me.

"That was a good transition, because I made the break from John Hancock and went out entirely by myself—and though it's not easy, I love it! Its great to be on your own, using the energy and talent you have inside in a positive way. And you don't have to watch your back or worry about who you have to please, like you do sometimes in a corporate environment. All you have to do is work towards building that business, and providing a good, positive environment for people to be happy in. You only have to please your clients and yourself.

"And I like to have a professional *and* personal relationship with clients. We've spent holidays together in many cases. They are very much a part of my life. They are not just commission in the bank for me. What I have in the bank is their trust and goodwill. But of course, people on the Street wonder how you're doing, and if you're going to survive, but I tend to thrive on that. You know, people love to call and say negative things either about the business or about the markets, but life goes on and you have to be positive, you always have to go forward."

Unfortunately, at this point, Maria had to go forward, so to speak, herself. The markets were still rocking, and she was needed back in the trenches. As we got up, she left me with what I thought were some appropriate parting words. "I love what I do," she said, her face beaming. "I have a lot of energy—I think I could work till I'm 100. No one is going to dictate to me when I'm going to retire. It's my call."

Bernadette Bartels Murphy

Chief Technical Analyst, Kimelman & Baird, LLC

New York has always been a magnet for dreamers and schemers eager to prove themselves in the most challenging—and rewarding—city in the world. Some make it, some don't. Looking out the window of money manager Bernadette Bartels Murphy's office, I thought briefly about the thousands of people swirling below me, each with their own dreams, each intent on carving a life for themselves out of the concrete; although they all look remarkably alike from so high up, each maybe harbors the secret belief that they will be one of the chosen few to rise above the teeming millions and find a place in the sun. It's incredible to think about where they all came from, what attracted them, and what's driving them now, as they jostle through traffic, flag down cabs, and disappear down subway

entrances. Only a few will reach the level of a Bernadette Murphy.
She has achieved the New York dream—the dream of the Street.

Whereas some people who have scraped and scrapped for years
in their drive to the top become hardened and self-absorbed,
Bernadette is notably lacking in bitterness and shares her good fortune through her activity in various charities and religious causes she
feels strongly about. Having made it, she's not turning her back on
the rest of the world.

Outside her darkly paneled office walls, Murphy has a host of
responsibilities besides managing money. A chartered market technician with years of experience unraveling the twists and turns of the
market, she has been a regular panelist on *Wall $treet Week with Louis
Rukeyser* for 17 years, as well as a frequent guest on CNBC and
CNN's *Moneyline*. She's built a reputation as a woman who can not
only navigate the markets successfully as a manager, but is also able
to effectively communicate the forces underlying market behavior.

Responsible for over $165 million in client money, Bernadette
is without question a highly visible member of the financial community. As far back as the 1970s, when she was first elected president
of the Financial Women's Association, Bernadette raised her profile,
networked, and expanded her sphere of influence through energetic
leadership in numerous professional societies and financial organizations. She served as the first woman president of the Market Technicians Association, and in the mid-1980s was elected president of the
New York Society of Security Analysts (at the time, only the second
woman to hold that post in the society's then 43-year history). She
also was elected to the board of directors of the Financial Analysts
Federation (and served as that organization's chairman in a second
term) and was a founding member of the International Society of
Financial Analysts. Most recently, she received the Distinguished
Service Award from the Association for Investment Management
and Research. All this on top of her analysis and consultation on be-

half of money managers at banks, trusts, insurance companies, mutual funds, pension funds, and high net-worth individuals.

But there's much more to her life than dollar figures, (no matter how impressive they may be) and professional recognition. Her success on the Street is simply one part of a full, rounded life. In her spare time she sits on corporate boards, financial advisory boards, and on the boards of religious organizations like Sacred Heart of Mary, Sisters of the Divine Compassion, and St. Paul's Benevolent Education and Missionary Institute.

Bernadette's career began in 1961 with a position in the corporate bond department at Landenburg, Thalmann & Company. One day early in her career, the stock and bond markets were plunging and traders were frantically trying to unload their positions. In the middle of this mayhem, there was one calm person, the financial officer of an insurance company, and he was *buying* convertible bonds. When Bernadette asked him how he acted so skillfully, he answered, "Technical analysis—the market has bottomed so it's time to get back in." Bernadette thought, *This is it, this is the edge I've been looking for.* She's been on the cutting edge ever since.

After graduating from college, it wasn't long before Bernadette found her way to Wall Street. She recalled, "The only reason I went to Wall Street at all was because of an uncle who had worked on the stock exchange as a college student. His enthusiasm prompted me to interview with a friend of his. Although I was immediately offered a job, I declined, because on second thought, Wall Street was the last place I saw myself working. But the office manager called me a number of times, and I finally said to myself, 'Well, I guess it's about time I learned something practical. I'll find out what Wall Street is all about.' At first, I didn't understand that world or what anybody was talking about. But after taking some courses, I began to find the financial arena fascinating. After two years, I was hooked."

When Bernadette started working at Ladenburg, Thalmann, & Company, she was the only woman in her department. When I asked her if that had been awkward, she shrugged it off and said, "Not really. I've always gotten along well with men. My boss started calling me by my last name rather than my first, and that seemed to take gender out of the equation. In fact, one of the first things my boss said to me was, 'Look, I'm going to give you a blanket apology right now for the language you're going to hear, and it's the only apology you'll get.' I said, 'Fine.' When I first heard my last name shouted out loud—'Bartels!'—I was startled. But I soon noticed that gender took a backseat at those moments, and I became just part of the team. It was like a button was pressed: gender neutral. When it was 'Bernadette,' I tended to sit back and defer to the men."

A woman with a mission, Bernadette was flatly determined to have a career before marrying and "settling down." Acknowledging the importance of her work, Bernadette explained, "I always felt I wanted to accomplish something. I wasn't quite sure what it would be, but I certainly knew that before I married I was going to accomplish *something*. That was my driving force. I wanted to be a fulfilled person, confident in myself, before I got married. My dad always encouraged me to explore, reach, and do as much as I could. His enthusiasm spurred me on. Having attended all-female schools gave me the gumption to speak out, not to be intimidated."

Bernadette stared out her office window, looking down at crowds of midmorning commuters, remembering, "Early on, my dad made a big impact on me. He always encouraged me to develop my mind. 'With a trained mind, you can do anything,' he'd say. He told me not to be in a hurry to get married—challenge the world and take advantage of it. Anybody can get married at any time, he cautioned. My uncle also had great confidence in me, and my first significant boyfriend was also supportive."

Bernadette did not plan on becoming a specialist in technical analysis, but the chance episode with her client impressed upon her the value of this approach. "I just stumbled onto it. I was on a convertible bond desk during one of the market declines of the 1960s. People were throwing stocks out the window; it was chaos. I thought, 'There has got to be a way to anticipate this. These are intelligent people and they're not acting in an intelligent manner. Why is that?'

"When prices dropped, we'd buy—and as they dropped further, we'd buy some more. We bought on a scale down, not on a scale up. My client, who was a chief financial officer, told me he was using technical analysis to pick his entry points, but back then, I had no idea what technical analysis was. So I took a course and started monitoring the market with my own charts."

As Bernadette's market knowledge developed, she began to branch out. "In the early 1970s, I was asked to track a portfolio for another insurance company, which I did. I realized that if I was going to monitor individual stocks, I also had to understand the structure of the market—the environment in which stocks traded. I started researching and writing about the stock market, and my readings were very accurate. During the 1973–1974 debacle, my timing was right, my anticipation of what was going to happen to stocks was on the money, so I started getting phone calls from institutions and invitations to lunch. And that's how my business began to build."

Analyst John Murphy once told me that when he first started charting and working at technical analysis, people in the office called it "voodoo" and "witchcraft." "Yes," Bernadette nodded, sinking back into her chair. "I hate those terms, but that's actually how people sometimes refer to it. What I've found fascinating is that with the advent of computers, quantitative analysts have adopted technical truths that have been used by technicians like me for years. Technical analysis has run into some distrust because there was a period of time, in the 1930s, when people abused it. Now chartered technicians have ethical standards that they must abide by, and they do."

Bernadette continued, "Technical analysis has become a major part of forecasting, actually a major part of any kind of analysis of the market, but at Kimelman & Baird, I always use it in conjunction with fundamental analysis. I make recommendations strictly on a technical basis, but I don't act unless both my partner, Sheila Baird, and I agree on the move. She's more of a fundamentalist than I am, and if we don't have consensus, we don't act."

Bernadette has seen her share of changes on the Street since she first entered finance. "Women have really come a long way," she said. "When I started in the business, the doors to the research department were not open to me. I had to take a path that was open, and that consisted of the trading markets and eventually technical analysis. Now those closed departments are more open to women. There's still a lot of discrimination, but we just accept it, keep a sense of humor, and work around it. Men also discriminate among *themselves.* It's a fact of life. Watching how men interact I realized that they had their own fraternity-style way of discriminating between those who were acceptable, and those who weren't. Questions such as, 'Where did you go to school?' 'Who did you marry?' 'Where do you live?' 'Who are your clients?' were used to establish hierarchies. If they are that discriminating among themselves, it just follows that you'd have to deal with even more discrimination as a woman.

"So how can a woman face something like that? By showing that she is knowledgeable, that she has a fine mind, that she can compete, that she can be depended upon to get the job done. Discrimination can be character building in that way. You must also keep a sense of humor and put things in perspective. A sense of humor is absolutely essential. Ours is a bottom-line business. If you can impact the bottom line of a company in a positive way, there is a place for you."

I mentioned Liz Bramwell's comment that being a woman has actually given her an edge in the investment field. Bernadette agreed. "I think that women have a greater sensitivity and awareness of people. Technicians must always follow the psychology of the market. That's always been a fascinating aspect to me—the environment that we're in at any particular time, how people are reacting, what they're doing. That's a big part of technical analysis. I learned over the years to weed out and stay with the tools that work. I use basic indicators that have been with me for years and that I depend upon, but I've also added some other bells and whistles that are unique to what I do and that I think have been instrumental in the reliability of the particular structure of my indicators."

It's easy to see why Bernadette is a productive analyst, given her daily routine. "There's a lot to do. Every morning, we print out the market diary that appears in the newspaper on spreadsheets. Then we do moving averages and ratios for the various numbers that are included in that. We have developed simple indicators. We utilize the ARMs Index, using various time frames, and do rates-of-change of market indices using a variety of time frames. We have all sorts of moving averages and spreads. Relative strength is extremely important in how a stock is responding to the market and to its group. We focus a lot on industry groups, and I try to maximize every day."

Murphy and her close friend Sheila Baird, who started out with Murphy in the business and is a founding partner of the firm Kimelman & Baird, LLC, joined forces to form a money management division in 1986. If all that weren't enough to fill her plate, Murphy also volunteers as a consultant to two orders of nuns and one order of priests. "I was raised Roman Catholic and, since I have been trained in finance, I feel that I can help them accomplish their goals as they helped me," she explained. "That's why I've done so much volunteer work in the industry."

Bernadette feels that women who want to have a career in finance should definitely concentrate on business courses in college. "I was a liberal arts major—history, English, and philosophy—and I loved it. Being a liberal arts major, when you come out of school, you have a trained mind and you're capable of accomplishing, but it takes you a while to put all the pieces together. I still love that part of my life, but in retrospect I think I would have emphasized the business part earlier. I would certainly have gone to graduate school—it's a shortcut to putting the pieces together because you're in a structured environment where you will learn how to solve the challenges you meet in business. I think that's very helpful and efficient. It will save time in your career."

Murphy believes that Wall Street is relatively gender blind. "It's so bottom-line oriented," she contended. "That's why I think it's a wonderful place for women to work. At the present time, the majority is still made up of men, but there's a gradual balance emerging. I think women with the proper aptitude and the will can make it in this industry. The bottom line that determines success for either a man or a woman is: 'Can you make money?' That, in essence, makes gender less relevant."

Thinking about how much she seems to take on in her professional life, I told Bernadette how hard it is for me to find time for my husband. She seemed to know exactly what I was talking about. "I marvel how anyone with a career has time to raise a family. In my age group, there were fewer of us who married. I eventually did marry in my 40s, but a great number of women in my network *never* married. I think it was just too tough. You couldn't possibly handle the job and the demands of a family without tremendous stress. If you did manage, you couldn't fit other people and other things into your life. Today managements are somewhat more understanding and make support systems for families available." But while Bernadette's work has been her driving force, luckily, her orthodontist husband, Dr. Eugene Murphy, understands and supports her.

Some of the women I've talked to feel that because there are more women on the Street now, they feel more pressure to make a visible impact as women. I mentioned to Bernadette that I don't know whether that's really a correct assumption on their part, or whether they should just try and stand out *period*. Bernadette replied, "That's a good point. To be successful, you definitely have to stand out, no matter who you are. You have to make a noticeable difference. Wall Street has accepted more women, but we are still a very small minority, particularly when it comes to leadership—so I think we have a double responsibility. We must be achievers *and* we must make a significant difference."

Bernadette has not only made a difference inside Wall Street. As everyone knows, in her spare time, she has made a difference as a financial advisor to a number of charities and religious organizations. "The people I work with in charities are just terrific because they're so dedicated, and they're always trying to do what's right for others. The biggest challenge is being able to provide for the retirement years of the older members of religious orders. I try to help them by choosing and monitoring solid investment managers who will protect their limited nest eggs."

I wound up the interview with a typical "Barbara Walters" question: "Would she do it all over again?" Bernadette paused, then replied thoughtfully, "Working on Wall Street does have its downside. It's exhausting, demanding, and extremely competitive. But, ultimately, it is very satisfying and I wouldn't trade it for any other job experience in the world. I love my work. Looking back, I might not do everything exactly the same way, but I wouldn't have missed this ride for anything. And for me, Wall Street has been the best. After all these years, I'm *still* not ready to get off!"

Elaine Garzarelli

President and CEO,
Garzarelli Investment Management

I had two hours to get to the restaurant, interview Elaine Garza-relli, and get back to the newsroom to make the afternoon show. I rushed out of the building into one of the worst snowstorms the East Coast had seen in 20 years with my producer running after me, demanding that I "ask her if the Dow will push past 6000. You know, we could use it on your show tonight." I screamed over the racket of the snowplows, "For the 10th time, Rich, this isn't that kind of interview. The only way anyone could predict something like that is to talk directly with God."

"Well, maybe Elaine does talk to God," he said, shivering. "I wouldn't put it past her to have that kind of a connection."

"If she does talk to God, Rich, I suspect she has other things to ask *Her* about."

As the cab pulled away from the curb, I tried to gather myself. When I'm about to do an interview, I need to relax, focus on the discussion at hand, and go over questions. This interview in particular already had me on edge—I was going to be talking with Elaine Garzarelli, one of the most brilliant minds on the Street. Have you ever had one of those days when you just felt overwhelmed? Well, I was running late, battling the snow, and also, admittedly, somewhat intimidated. *Elaine Garzarelli*—I wanted to be on top of my game.

If there is anyone on Wall Street seemingly destined to be a player from birth, it would have to be Elaine Garzarelli. She brings to mind a female version of Alex Keaton from *Family Ties*—a serious, studious young person with little time for play but always time for the *Wall Street Journal*. I imagined her poring over the family finances with her parents, guiding them through home loans and investment strategies.

My picture of Elaine as a young girl was not quite accurate, but it did have some elements of truth to it. Growing up, she didn't spend much time playing with friends. Her mother would even go so far as to put notes on the front door informing the other kids that Elaine wasn't available. But instead of reading stock tables or performing advanced calculus, she was studying chemistry or furiously practicing piano, her real interests at the time. Her mother insisted on "business" first—socializing could come later.

Mother's wisdom paid off. Today, Elaine is known as the "Guru of Wall Street," a title that doesn't seem to affect her much one way or the other, but has a great impact on everyone else on Wall Street. Elaine Garzarelli commands attention. Why? Because she excels at her craft, and quite frankly, is usually right about the stock market, a gift that has earned both her clients and her employers millions of dollars. What E. F. Hutton's commercials claimed in the '70s, Elaine made a reality in the '80s and '90s: When Elaine speaks, *everybody* on Wall Street listens.

Like most people I've met in this business, Elaine didn't discover her true calling until she was in college. "Growing up, I wanted to be a chemical engineer or chemist," Elaine explained. "I went to Drexel University for two reasons: It was my father's alma mater and had a reputation for being one of the top chemistry schools in the country. Also, it was located in Philadelphia, near where my parents live. My brother was attending Penn and the two schools are adjacent. In my freshman year, I enrolled in an elective economics course. I understood it better than I had understood anything in my life. It just came naturally to me. My friends found it hard to pick it up and understand why saving is bad and spending is good. I understood right away that if you get the money out and working, it picks up momentum, multiplies, accelerates. It was easy for me to grasp these concepts. The whole world is based on economics: wars are based on economics, our personal lives are based on economics. The subject is fascinating and all-encompassing. Happily, I switched my major."

It's rather mind-boggling to think about what Elaine accomplished at such an early age. She started working at Drexel Burnham Lambert while still in college. In her early 20s, she was assigned to research stock price fluctuations. And what did this prodigy come back with? Not the humdrum paper hundreds of finance students had submitted before and since. Elaine Garzarelli came back with an entirely new theory of how Wall Street works. Think about that for a second. Elaine was not yet out of her 20s, and she redefined Wall Street at a time when there weren't many women even working there. Elaine's theory belonged to a branch of financial theory known as econometrics—the science of relating the economy mathematically to factors that influence its direction.

When I asked Elaine about her first professional assignment, she cringed a bit but laughed at the memory. "My first six-month assignment turned into a 12-year project! Drexel charged me to find out what makes the stock market go up and down, and how the economy is directly related to this up and down movement. I had six months to do it. At that time, everybody on Wall Street was a market technician: I wanted to do something groundbreaking and based on fundamentals. Econometrics was a brand new science in 1972. I had the first IBM 360 computer on Wall Street, but even with the new computer, I felt I had just scratched the surface after six months. Nothing made sense yet. I found that when the economy was booming, that was the best time to sell and when the economy was horrible, that was the time to buy. I could not fathom it. I tried hundreds of correlations and after twelve years, I finally figured it out! When the economy is peaking, it's bad; when it's bottoming, it's good."

I asked Elaine how her research findings have affected her methods of prediction. As she explained, "Significant evaluations have to do with cash flow and operating earnings, not reported earnings, which is what most of the people on Wall Street look at. Sentiment, which gauges the degree of optimism or pessimism of market participants at different points in the market, is a contrary indicator that we added about eight years ago because of our research results. It pays to be skeptical when market opinion is at either positive or negative extremes. Prior to that, we used three other indicators to pick every major turn in the market. This new system goes against the norm. I found that when everyone else was negative about the market, I was positive. I was against the consensus at turning points, but I gained confidence as I went along. I used to feel anxious because I was telling all my clients to buy at a time when this was going against established 'wisdom.' I was often quite nervous because of the amount of money I was dealing with, but the second, third, and fourth times I got buy signals, I followed the indications without hesitation. Now I know what I'm supposed to feel is directly opposite the norm, so it doesn't alarm me."

Most successful people can pinpoint a turning point in their profession. In my own career in newscasting, it was the day a TV producer ran into my office, tossed six pages of news on my desk, and announced, "You are going on live in five minutes." I wasn't sure if I was grateful or horrified. Of course I was terrified, but I made it through the ordeal in one piece. Elaine told me that a similar incident happened to her in 1982. She predicted that the bear market was over and that we were entering a bull market. From that point on, her colleagues really started to listen to her. Unfortunately, most didn't want to hear what she had to say one morning in 1987. Yes, they were listening, but they weren't paying attention.

Monday, October 19, 1987—no financial reporter will ever forget that day. As the world rotated on its axis and opening bells rang first on one stock exchange and then another, the shock waves swept around the globe. From Hong Kong to Singapore to London and then New York, it was indeed "Black Monday." As night settled, nearly everyone in the market was reeling. The numbers were staggering: U.S. companies experienced losses in excess of $500 billion in a single day. Elaine Garzarelli, who was working as a market strategist for Shearson Lehman at the time, had predicted the crash to mostly deaf ears.

Why? Because most analysts on Wall Street are in love with the industries they cover; they become "attached" to automotives, transportations, food stuffs, retailing, and so on. This engagement made it difficult for Elaine to convince them that their "babies" were heading for a nosedive. At research meetings, Garzarelli would announce, "We're going into a serious recession." She was met with looks of disbelief and disgust. One of the auto analysts hotly responded, "What the hell are you talking about? You're going too far this time." She told him, "Listen, the economy overpowers everything. If the economy goes down, I don't care how good management is. Margins are going to get squeezed and companies are going to underperform." She illustrated this mathematically by correlating interest rates to auto sales, housing sales, and every other relevant industry. Analysts pointed to a hundred other indicators they had looked at, and only six or seven even correlated to the industries in question. She explained, "Analysts were so in love with their industries or companies, they would follow indicators that had no relevance, and they didn't even know they were being unduly emotional about it."

Back when I was a news reporter, I vividly recall Elaine boldly sitting in front of the television cameras and predicting the crash. I remember thinking, *Oh, my god, that's got to take guts to say!* That was a ballsy move, I told Elaine. How did you know for sure?

"The writing seemed to be there," she answered. "All my financial indicators turned negative in September when the Fed raised the discount rate, then the Japanese bond market crashed and I just knew the time had come. A few TV shows called us, but I didn't go on any of them. I wanted to be completely sure. By October 13th, things looked so bad that I agreed to do an interview with *USA Today*. Then, Lou Dobbs asked me to come on CNN's *Moneyline* on October 13, 1987, and I agreed. I remember walking over to the studio with a broker friend of mine and saying, 'What am I going to say to Lou Dobbs? Things look so bad.' She said, 'Just tell it like it is. We all want to know what to do.' I replied, 'Lehman's going to kill me.' Instead of saying 'It's going to be a Bear market but things will be O.K., don't worry,' I said, 'It's going to collapse.' My indicators were pointing to a scenario every bit as bad as in 1929. They had dropped to 8 percent and anything below 30 is a major sell signal. Lou Dobbs gaped and almost fell off his chair. No one realized I was *that* negative. In September I had made a negative report calling for a Bear market, but this was the first time I had been so negative 'live' on television."

But those who listened to Elaine and took her advice were spared considerable pain and misery. "Yes, that was a good feeling," Elaine agreed. "The good news was that my fund went up 5 percent that day and the market went down 35 percent. The *Wall Street Journal* picked that up and wrote a large article. I got credit for predicting the crash. If I had made that call on TV and the fund had not performed the way it did, I probably would not have received as much credit."

I once read an article about how antilock brakes override human reactions. The brake system anticipates the driver's natural reaction and does the opposite, similar to the way Elaine reacts to the stock market. "Good moves are anticipatory," Elaine explained. "That's why when things look great, you sell. When things look horrible, you buy."

Elaine also called the turnaround in 1988. Poring over a list of market variables, including interest rates, economic indicators, and corporate earnings, she got a buy signal in February 1988 and informed Shearson's clients that the bull was back.

"It has always been an uphill battle because analysts would beg me not to downgrade their industries, telling me that their management was especially good and to look at this or that. Sometimes I wouldn't go into the office in order to avoid them and began to work in a vacuum." Shortly thereafter Elaine stopped going into the office entirely and discovered the value of working away from the distractions of the office. Now she works out of her home in Boca Raton, Florida—a rough setting most of us would no doubt envy. It would be easy to envision Elaine lounging poolside in a long, flowing caftan, with a cell phone in hand and a pitcher of fruit punch on a nearby table. But I know better. Even if the image were partially true, there would also be piles of research reports and computer printouts strewn about, in addition to the obligatory laptop sitting on the table.

"Fifteen years ago I began working at home," Elaine told me. "Two weeks a month, I'm like a hermit—I just work. I talk to about 50 economists a month in different industries and use my econometrics model to process the input I get from them on pricing, inventories, exports, things like that. They talk shop to me in a way that they don't talk to analysts or the people who recommend stocks. They talk to me as a buddy, so I'm getting unique and valuable information. Our work has beaten the majority consensus the last 12 years in a row."

I commented that as a newscaster, I am, of course, surrounded by nonstop activity. Television stations are not quiet places and interruptions abound. "That's exactly why I work at home," Elaine said. "I really enjoyed going into the office. We had a great time; it was a party every day. But I would be right in the middle of an econometric model and someone would pop a champagne cork because it was a birthday or someone had adopted a baby. I would drink the champagne, of course, and wouldn't be able to think clearly from that point on. And then there would be cake. That was everyday life on Wall Street. I really couldn't get much work done, but I enjoyed it. In this sense, research is a lot different than the trading floor where it's possible to get the job done and socialize a bit more. As a result, I did all my work on the weekends and at night. But, as time went on, I really wanted to get my work done during the day so I could have somewhat of a life after hours. Now, when I have a free day to play, I go into the office."

Market analysts are known for being private, often eccentric individuals. Elaine described the benefits of finding her niche. "I could never be a salesperson. I'm doing what I'm best suited to do—research. You should see some of the research people. If they were in sales, they'd never even get to first base. Brilliant minds, but no social grace whatsoever. One fellow analyst would always come to work carrying a large suitcase. His clothes were always in tatters. His office was right next to mine and it was a filthy mess. It smelled strange, too. He'd wear the same exact clothes for three days in a row. I still wonder what was really in that suitcase. But, that's the kind of person who's in research. I'm not a corporate kind of person. I hate to go to meetings or sit still for too long. I don't mind being on a telephone conference call because if a meeting drags on you can tune out and get other work done or pace about. But, meetings in general tend to drag on and on. No, I'm happy doing what I do."

As a result of the infamous *Wall Street Journal* profile, Elaine was dubbed the "Guru of Wall Street." Naturally, most people do not view themselves in the same light as the media views them. When asked how she felt about the title, Elaine laughed heartily. "I absolutely do not think of myself that way, I just think of myself as a good analyst, but I am happy to take the credit because I feel that I have produced good work for many years. I have been in the business since 1972 and made many correct calls prior to predicting the crash of 1987, and I've made more than a few accurate calls since. It was a good feeling to be right on in a big way in 1987, especially because it impressed my mother. She loved it. She had previously warned, 'Elaine, don't talk about such high numbers. Don't stick your neck out all the time; hedge your bets.' She was always trying to tell me what to do to protect myself. I told her, 'I can't stand hedging and won't do it for anybody.' I am pretty aggressive in the things that I say and that's one of the reasons I get noticed. Admittedly, it also helps to be right and make money for clients."

I wanted to know just how much of her decision making is based on an exact system and how much is plain old gut feeling. She explained that her system accounts for about 50 percent of a decision. While she built the system herself, she still needs to fly it well each time, and that takes a certain amount of hands-on feel.

"I need to be able to predict earnings and cash flow, interest rates, when the Fed's going to ease up," explained Elaine. "The gut part has a lot to do with how much I feel that market is anticipating the economy. I get that sense through talking with my institutional clients. It used to be that your earnings peaked and the market peaked at the same time. Now, earnings peak after the market peaks. So each cycle is different and prediction has become more sophisticated. Sometimes the cycles are in sync and it's not difficult. You have to keep track of how the institutions are thinking and then put a little of your gut into it in terms of timing."

We've all met super-successful individuals who seem downright insular, not only keeping to themselves, but keeping others, especially the talented or sharp, at arms length. Elaine, however, surrounds herself with the best and brightest. Elaine began developing strong professional relationships when she was only 21 years old by collecting business cards at National Association of Business Economists meetings. "And I've been collecting business cards ever since. I follow up and it has produced results. I'm now working closely with some of the best economists in the country."

Several of the big firms have tried to seduce her research assistants in an effort to gather intelligence about how Elaine's system works. "Several firms have tried to hire my assistants, increased their salaries significantly, and asked them to reproduce my work," she laughed. "Of course, they didn't realize the task it is and went off into other fields. It takes time and experience and, frankly, it's not all that easy. It's very complex and requires a combination of skills. You have to understand what clients are thinking, what the consensus is, and when to go against the consensus. Contacts with top economists take years to develop, and then you've got to know the biases of those economists. You need to establish a relationship where they will talk easily with you. You get to know the areas in which they're good and bad. You get to know where they're emotional and where they're level-headed. Then, you've got to use the model, the structure. You have to sense when the growth stocks or price-earning ratios are going to expand. You have to look at history, but then you've got to see that now things are a little different. For instance, earnings-growth and GDP growth are going to be slow because of population changes, growth in the labor force, and aging of the population. Companies like Coca-Cola and those in the food industry should have higher multiples because of emerging markets. But historically, if you look at the old models, you'd say those companies were over-valued. You have to have the judgment and foresight to discern that we're going to experience expansion in certain areas. It's going to be like 1950 all over again, but slightly different."

Elaine's shift into the world of self-employment was not entirely her own decision. As a result of salary disputes and fundamental disagreement about the economic outlook, Lehman and Elaine parted company. Elaine took four months off to travel Europe and sort things out.

For the past 10 to 15 years, we've been inundated with articles in the press and bits on television magazine shows showing how successful women balance their careers and their family. We've been told again and again that we too can "have it all." The reality, as most of us well know, is that while some superwomen may pull it off, most of us aren't capable of giving the job 200 percent and coming home to cook for the husband and change the baby's diaper. We make choices about where we're going to commit most of our time and energy. But, most of us don't acknowledge the reality of the situation, at least not publicly. Elaine was brutally honest in this regard. "I don't really have a normal life. My significant other is my work and I'm very passionate about it. I have a dog and good friends. I also have a boyfriend, Doug, who understands because he is also an economist and econometrician. We've been dating for 15 years and have a ball when we're together. We've decided that we'll get married when we're about 65. We're not going to have kids, so there's really no reason to get married now. For companionship, we may tie the knot when we're older. My personal assistant is also my best friend. Right now, she's taking care of my dog and answering the phone while I'm away. Doug has his own company in New York but he comes down to Florida for weekends or I go to New York. I play the piano and love music, especially Pavarotti. After I finish my reports or two weeks of living like a hermit, I blast the music."

Elaine's mornings consist of sit-ups, leg bends, and report writing before she gets going on her new work. She wastes no time. "There used to be so much time lost just getting ready to go to the office," she remembered. "I had to think about make-up, stockings, clothing, high heels, a purse that matches, hair, jewelry. I used to be lucky to get a monthly report done in a month. At home, I can work in the middle of the night, at five in the morning, or whenever I want. I can work whenever I get the urge. I need to move around a lot, so it's important for me to exercise and stretch after sitting for an hour or two. When I have to think about something, I go for a run. My whole life is integrated this way now."

When Elaine started in the business she was the only woman in her department, but the writing was clearly on the wall for her. The top people at Drexel knew they had a winner. Her early research findings were a hint of brilliant predictions to come. But she had other hurdles to clear: She was 21, attractive if not downright striking, and bright. Her male colleagues treated her very well, but there was a problem—clients wouldn't believe anything she told them. *What can she know at 21?* they probably wondered. This is a joke! Instead, they would flirt with her as if she were a kid. They just couldn't take seriously anything this young woman had to impart—especially regarding earnings analysis. It wasn't until she was about 33 that clients began to really listen to her forecasts. In the office, her colleagues had paid attention from the beginning—she was right all the time. But it took quite a while for the sales force and clients to really believe in her. Growing older and more mature, making the *Institutional Investor* All-Star Team in 1983 for 11 consecutive years, and sticking her neck out for her beliefs were collectively what it took to prove herself. Elaine pushed herself and pushed those with whom she worked to believe in her all the time.

And once you understand where Elaine has come from, you appreciate why she drives herself so hard. Going back to that young girl with the insistent mother, we find that the constant admonition in the early years was to study, study, study. It doesn't take a therapist to see that the adult Elaine has translated this into work, work, work. "My mother would make us read a book a day all through childhood. In the summer, she'd expect us to do one experiment a day in the chemistry laboratory downstairs, take elocution lessons, play the piano, all kinds of things that we didn't have time to do during the school year. We were hardly ever allowed to play in the traditional sense. She said that the most important thing was to get straight As and to develop our minds—to be brilliant in our endeavors. She wouldn't let me do a lot of the things that most other kids did. For instance, I had to beg her to let me play basketball. She thought that once you'd developed intellectually, there would be time to be social. That comes naturally. Mom told us that we could always go to parties, have friends, develop social skills." Especially once you have made it on Wall Street.

Today Elaine is an established presence on the Street. She doesn't necessarily have to go to the mat for what she believes in, but there are times when business associates still question her calls. Just before the Gulf War in September 1990, the director of Shearson asked her, "Are you sure you got a buy signal? How could this be? We haven't even won the war." She replied, "I feel sick in the stomach because I feel it's a buy signal—but it's definitely a buy signal." He asked, "How do you know who's going to win the war?" Elaine responded, "I don't care who's going to win the war. The market is down 20 percent, it's undervalued, interest rates have come down, we're in the middle of a recession. It's simply the best time to buy." Elaine turned out to be right. The market did drop for a few more days, then shot up. That turned out to be one of her best market calls—better than the 1987 crash call, she believes.

Knowing what she knows now, and remembering how hard she worked—and is still working—would she do it the same way again? I asked. "Absolutely. If I died tomorrow, I wouldn't want my mother, or brother, or friends to mourn. I would want them to celebrate my life. I've had a lot of glory. I've had a lot of fun. I've traveled the world: Jakarta, Singapore, Hong Kong, Japan, Europe. I've enjoyed first class treatment at Lehman—private jet, the whole nine yards. It's been wonderful. I've gotten some bad press, my fund had a bad year and it broke my heart, but that goes along with the territory. You can't avoid hitting a few potholes once in a while on the road. So, I would definitely say that I'd do it again. I'd do it a thousand times over!"

Elaine as of this writing was bullish, as she's been all year, even given the fact that many market commentators have been skeptical, if not downright scared, as the Dow continues to break new highs. But knowing Elaine Garzarelli's track record, you'd be crazy not to consider her forecast.

Linda Bradford Raschke

LBR Group

In a way, it might seem like the classic 1980s story: A young college graduate is drawn to the fledgling equity options markets in the early part of the decade, gets a seat to trade on an exchange floor, and starts raking in money as the bull market takes off.

And if that was the real story, or the end of the story, it might apply to any number of young mavericks who swarmed to the trading floors in the go-go decade, thrusting once murky concepts of "options" and "futures" into the public consciousness. But for money manager Linda Bradford Raschke, it was only the beginning of the story, one that took a painful twist almost out of the gate when she blew out after only three months of trading, leaving her, at age 23, in debt tens of thousands of dollars to her clearing firm.

While this kind of experience probably would have knocked most people out of the ring for good, for Linda it was the first step of a market journey that culminated in her present position as a successful futures fund manager and recognition as a top trader in Jack Schwager's *New Market Wizards.* When I interviewed her, she had just published a book on the markets, *Street Smarts* (one of the few trading books by a woman you'll see on the market), and was one of the most sought-after speakers on the trading circuit. Everyone wants to know how Linda trades.

Although she has attained a rare level of success in her field and is one of the friendliest and most accessible high-profile traders in the business, Linda has a strong sense of privacy and actually plans to "go underground," as she puts it, in the not-too-distant future. She's not even accepting more money for her funds. Not for her is the ego-gratifying spotlight that for so many big-name traders seems to be their second priority in life after money. Her focus lies elsewhere: in doing quality work, in her family, in building a business for the long haul.

I set out early one Saturday morning to drive to Linda's southern New Jersey home. Contrary to popular stereotypes, New Jersey is quite a beautiful state (once you get past the industrial part of the turnpike), and my drive through rolling woods and farmland was a relaxing one. When I finally found Linda's house in a private and wooded area, I was greeted by her husband Skip, who told me Linda had just left with their seven-year-old daughter, Erika, for the nearby stables to indulge in Linda's one passion outside trading: horses. We decided to drive over together and meet them there.

Linda takes her riding seriously. When she isn't trading, she's on a horse. I watched her for most of the morning, and her total concentration and confidence were palpable—the same single-mindedness she brings to her endeavors in the markets.

Back at the house, though, I wasn't really thinking about trading. Linda's home, apart from an office filled with the requisite computer terminals and charts, is about as far removed from the Street as you could imagine. Sitting in her living room by a crackling fireplace with jazz humming softly in the background, Skip, Erika, and an excitable Dalmatian named Axle all weaved in and out, lending a relaxed and casual feeling to the interview. It was easy to forget that a few steps away is the command center from which Raschke trades her own money—and $30 million in customer funds—in the futures markets.

Mention Linda's name to anyone who has met her and chances are they'll tell you what a nice person she is—it's practically a universal assessment. Her inviting personality and engaging smile can make you forget this is an ex–floor trader who noted market analyst and commentator John Murphy called "the best trader in the world." She didn't get that way by accident, and her story paints a portrait of a supremely driven, focused woman.

As soon as Axle settled down, we talked a little bit about beginnings. Linda saw her path as the natural outgrowth of her upbringing, although she initially had no specific plans.

"My dad has always been an entrepreneur," she explained, "a builder, and you just see this way of life—markets, being in business for yourself—there's good years and bad years, and you don't really know any other way. And I was always interested in the stock market because it seemed like an entrepreneurial way to make money. When I was at Occidental College, they had a program called the Blythe Fund, where 12 students were nominated to the board of directors and would actually manage the real dollars in the portfolio.

"We had all kinds of materials and our own broker in downtown Los Angeles, so I got some familiarity with the markets that way. At the time, I was studying music, which I got my degree in. But I didn't want to make a living that way—I did it just because I had always been good at playing piano and I loved it. So I also got a degree in economics, which I liked too. When I finished school I thought, 'Well, I'll be a stockbroker. I've certainly got four years of work experience.' " She shook her head. "But the rest of the world doesn't see it that way."

Relocating to San Francisco, Linda "actually applied to every brokerage office in the city, thinking, 'Well, one of them has to take me, right?' Wrong. Nobody hired me. The closest I came was actually considering taking a job with a life insurance company, because then you can still get your license to sell stock. I ended up getting an accounting type of position with a local San Francisco company.

"Something rather curious came of the experience, though. Several years later, I was contacted by an attorney regarding my application to one of the brokerage houses. Apparently, a class action discrimination suit was being filed on behalf of all female employees and job applicants. I was asked to verify my address and to confirm that I had applied for a job as a broker at a certain time. I signed the paperwork and returned it. I didn't think much of it. Several years later, however, just as I was preparing to move to Philadelphia, I received a check for $3,000 as a settlement. I couldn't believe it! At the time I didn't have much money and was trying to move across country and then here arrives this big check just because I'd applied to a certain brokerage house and not been hired!"

Her entrée to the trading floor came about courtesy of an options trader on the Pacific Coast Stock Exchange whom Linda met through playing tennis. "I asked him, 'Can you explain how you price options?' " Linda recalled, "and he showed me a little model with about six variables which sounded pretty simple, and I thought, 'Well, I can do that.'

"So I just started going down to the floor. The trading hours on the West Coast are tied to New York, so I could go down to the floor and watch the opening because I didn't have to be at my regular job until 8:30 A.M. I used to hang out and watch what these people did. There was a series of videotapes you could watch through First Options of Chicago on how to price options, and I thought, if they can do it, I can do it—not knowing at all what I was getting into, having no clue of the dangers of these highly leveraged products. My friend offered to back me as a trader, and I thought, 'Well, why not?' At the time, I was planning on getting an MBA."

Although I thought it unusual for a trader to back someone so inexperienced, Linda explained that it was fairly commonplace at the time: Traders would parlay their success by setting up other traders they thought had potential. If the new traders made money, the backer took a share of the profits. The only risk, Linda noted, was if one of the new traders "blew out." Little did she know she was about to join the ranks of this unfortunate group.

"The first three months I did very, very well," Linda said slowly, "and then I got caught in a takeover situation where the company got taken over at a much higher price than we all thought it would. We knew there was a takeover risk, but in those days if a stock was trading at 32, it might get taken over at 46. In this particular case, the bid came in twice as high as anybody had expected and the stock actually opened up at 66. I blew out, and just about everybody on the exchange floor who was trading the stock blew out or took a very hard hit. Keep in mind that I'm a very young kid, 23 years old at this point, and all of a sudden I go from having just made $25,000 in the last three months to suddenly losing $70,000 overnight, and in debt to my clearing firm $45,000."

My first inclination might have been to move back in with my parents and lick my wounds, I said. What did you do? "What can you do?" Linda asked, throwing her hands in the air. "You can't do anything. I cried a lot: 'I can't believe this happened to me!' I remember thinking, 'Boy, I could have had a Stanford MBA for this price.' That's how I looked at it. To me, the debt looked like a mountain so high I was never going to reach the top of it. There was nobody who could help me out of it. My backer also lost a half million in the same deal. He didn't have the money to back me again, he just barely had enough to keep trading himself.

"The only person in my family who had any money was my grandfather who had his own law firm up in Seattle, and he came down and kind of 'tsk tsk'ed' me. He came from a family of 12 kids where you made your own way, and his attitude was 'You bad girl, playing around with these financial markets. I can't help you out of this kind of trouble, you have to learn to work your way out of these situations yourself.' So, I had to make an arrangement with my clearing firm to pay back $1,000 every month for the next five years."

What a lesson, I thought, noticing a trace of incredulity in Linda's remembrance of her grandfather's stoic response in her time of need. As she recounted her feelings, some of the bewilderment that she must have felt at the time resurfaced, and she made it clear that this was one lesson she didn't need to learn.

"It was sort of like, wait a minute, I just graduated from college, I have all these student loans—in your 20s aren't you supposed to stop living like a student? I felt like I was set back about four years because all the extra money I made had to pay off this stupid disaster. And I'm probably the only one who paid back 100 percent on the dollar," Linda continued, sounding more than a little annoyed. "I found out later that all kinds of traders had negotiated deals with the clearing firms, paying 60 cents on the dollar. Because these traders paid so much in commissions to the clearing firms, it was more profitable for the clearing firms to keep the traders in business." She laughed. "Well old dummy here didn't know any better."

Linda waited for a moment, taking measure of the experience. "You know, you don't have to learn lessons like that in life. It was *more* than a lesson, it was about three years of being miserable and feeling like a slave with a ball and chain around my neck. Suddenly, you're doing what you're doing not because you love it and it's fun but because you have absolutely no choice and no other way in the world to pay back this kind of money."

Almost as an afterthought, she seemed to extract at least one positive from the ordeal. "It was a very, very miserable time in my life," she said, "but it's sort of why, I think, I can stand the business now. You go through experiences like this and the pain from bad trades seems like nothing compared to the pains you suffered earlier. It all becomes a relative thing.

"Also, you get used to having a very long time horizon. The way I perceive things in our personal lives and business lives—which are integrated—are in seven- to eight-year cycles of troughs and peaks. You'll have a great four to five years and then you might enter a three-year dip. You really step back and observe your life as this huge macrocycle."

Spoken like a true trader. That's an amazing way to look at it, I told her. I think that's the kind of experience where you either sink or swim, and you obviously swam. Was it something you found you really loved even after you paid off the debt? Linda shrugged. "By the time I paid it off when I was around 27, I thought, 'Well, I don't really know how to do anything else.' Suddenly, getting an MBA seemed so trivial in light of what I'd gone through. You see things in business and trading that sort of trivialize everything else. I felt like 'Wait a minute, I'm going to sit in a classroom and do quadratic equations—for what purpose?' It's too abstract.

"I'd seen a lot of MBAs come down to the trading floors, and they were kind of like sheep among the wolves—you know, 'Bring 'em on down!' They think the world will function like this nice little model or equation, and nothing's further from the truth. I think that an MBA can give you a false sense of security that you can use these mathematical models as sort of a crutch. It's amazing how many of the very successful entrepreneurs and businessmen in this world don't have college degrees. They haven't had a formal education telling them things shouldn't be done a particular way."

Linda, I knew, traded options on the floors of both the Pacific Stock Exchange and the Philadelphia Stock Exchange—one of the few women I've met who started out on the floor. Trading pits are an extreme expression of the traditional male dominance in the financial world. They have more than their fair share of ex-athletes, because physical stamina and quick reflexes are as crucial to success as market acumen. Floor traders are notorious for their independence, abrasiveness, and animosity to anything that disrupts the status quo.

Linda is a slender, attractive woman—she doesn't look like the type to go, literally, shoulder-to-shoulder with the pit crowd. But when I asked her what it was like, I was rather surprised to find that the popular perception of the floor as pure, adrenalized chaos didn't seem to hold true, at least not from Linda's initial experience on the smaller Pacific Coast exchange.

"I was first down on the trading floor back in 1981 and 1982 before the big bull market, and truthfully, it was pretty dull," she admitted. "We would usually go down on the floor for about an hour, open all the contracts, and then everybody would go out for breakfast. Then we'd sit upstairs for about another hour and watch the markets and wait until things picked up towards the end of the day, and then you'd go back down on the floor and stand there for an hour, and that was it. That's how it was originally—a relaxed environment, if you will."

I asked her if it was different because she was a woman. While I've noticed a tendency of some of the women I've interviewed to downplay discrimination (if not actually deny its existence), Linda seemed even more inclined than most to reject such notions, and to dismiss those who might say their gender made things difficult for them.

"I never personally saw it as being different," she said quickly. "There were three or four other women, and I think they felt the same way. Part of the reason is that we were all friends with the guys; we'd barbecue at each other's houses and play softball together." Linda had to take a moment (actually, several moments) to shoo Axle out of the living room before she could continue. "Quite frankly, it helps just as much as some people would say it hurts. Some people might go out of their way to help you out a little bit because you're female. On the other hand, there were just flagrant assholes who might get in your face, but it's not because you're female—they're that way to everybody. So, if you chose to take it personally, that it's because you're a woman, I think you were barking up the wrong tree. There are certain people out there who might have a victim mentality or a martyr mentality for whatever reason, and it's not a successful attitude."

That's encouraging to hear, I said, because I'd talked to other women—Bernadette Murphy's one of them, and Mary Farrell and Liz Mackay—who felt as though they had to work twice as hard as any man, that they were judged differently. But it sounds like you didn't really feel that.

"Well, maybe it's because trading is such a bottom-line business," Linda noted. "I'm not working for the judgment of my peers, I'm working for the bottom line, and nobody can argue whether you're successful or not if you've made money. That's all there is to it. Going through life, you can always choose to see the glass as half full or half empty. Whether you turn a particular situation into an asset or a liability is totally up to you. It doesn't matter if you're a woman or a Vietnam vet, it's all your attitude. Simply believing that you can do something is 95 percent of what it takes. It's a confidence thing, being able to see in your mind that it's going to happen. It far outweighs even how hard you work. You have to visualize the end goal. You just chip away at it, one step at a time, and don't worry about all the steps in the meantime because if you do, it will keep you from getting there.

"You can't bother along the way, worrying about 'Well, am I going to get discriminated against.' or 'Is it going to matter if I'm a woman.' Those things are ultimately so petty in the big scheme of things—you won't get anywhere worrying about them. You could also say there's a place for both women and men, and that they can offer very different things. It's part of a balanced perspective, a yin and yang, and it's important to have both views presented."

Up to this point, Linda hadn't talked about when or how she made the transition from floor trader to "upstairs" trader, a move that is notoriously difficult and often results in the trader leaving the business or returning to the floor. I asked Linda why she made the switch. "After San Francisco, I worked on the trading floor in Philadelphia, but in '87 I had a [horse] riding accident, and I had to leave the floor temporarily because I couldn't even stand up. Once I was upstairs I thought, 'Oh, I can do this from upstairs, too.' At this point I still had a backer, and I was trading his money. After a year, I went out on my own.

"Did I like it?" Linda mused. "It was okay." She paused again, as if weighing the pros and cons. "I think, initially, because it was my own money, I didn't want to risk it." She laughed. "I had seen so many people make money and give it back, make money and give it back. Initially it was hard to make bets with my own money. But, no risk, no gain.

"I still have a very difficult time. I don't even put my own personal money in the stock market, it's all sitting there in short-term T-bills—I'm not even going to risk it in the bond market!" she joked. "Actually, that's my nest egg money that I'm referring to. But I do have about 90 percent of my net worth in my own funds. I'm actually one of my largest clients, so I can truly say I do put my money where my mouth is. But it's a lot easier for me not to think about that money; it's very abstract, and I don't even count it as my own. I hope it grows because I hope I trade well."

Linda now has over $30 million in customer funds among three pools and two managed accounts. Surprisingly, she is not interested in taking on more money: She is satisfied where she is ("I'm trying to keep my business small"), feeling she can get the best performance for her clients this way. By contrast, many money managers seem to take secret (or not so secret) pride in having the biggest fund on the block.

Also, Linda has always traded for herself, and despite her rough start, has been successful. Many individual traders, especially floor traders, have difficulty making the transition to money manager. Linda went from floor trader to off-floor trader, to trading for herself, and then to trading other people's money. I asked her why she made the change and if she found it any more stressful or frustrating than personal trading.

"You've got to create your own challenges. Just trading for yourself, quite frankly, gets kind of boring after a while—I'd been doing it for 14 years. I had always wanted to see if I could run a certain kind of program. I saw the performance of a lot of people and thought, 'Hmm . . . I can do better than that.' I also wanted to create a more stable, long-term business that could carry us for the next 20 years. For a long time I had just traded for myself in an environment with nobody else around—that's actually probably why I did well, I didn't have anybody else's opinions getting in the way—but at some point I thought, 'Okay, enough of being a total hermit.' I found that I liked interacting with other people, I got a lot of satisfaction out of that. And it's nice to build a business you can be proud of, and do it from scratch and say, 'Look, I made something where there was once nothing.'

"It's not that it's a lot of pressure," she continued. "What I'm doing now I really perceive as running a business, which involves an entirely different set of responsibilities. I see myself as 'feeding the chain': I have people that work for me, I feed accountants, I feed attorneys, I feed brokers. And actually, I like that feeling—it's one of the benefits of being successful that I never really thought about. It's almost like, if you trade for yourself, in some respects, it's kind of selfish: 'I'll just keep my business and my thoughts to myself and not give to the system.' "

Linda shifted in her seat and smiled. "But on the other hand, trading for yourself is a very nice, nonstressful way of living. If I'm trading my own money, I can take off if I feel like it—I can go ride a horse, or do whatever I want. It was definitely nice at the time.

"But in the long run, you become aware of your own mortality: In your 20s, you don't think about that, but now I know ultimately I'm going to be in the grave, so I've got to pass on as much as I can to my children, or other people—" Linda cut herself off for a moment, and when she spoke again, she was laughing, her voice rising, as she seemed to realize exactly what she was talking about. "Maybe it's a little bit premature for me to start talking this way, because I'm only 37!"

Maybe. But then Linda told me a story that shed some light on these reflections and helped explain her outlook on life. It seems that at one point in her life, her "I can do anything and everything" philosophy got the best of her. "Well, I really went through a bad period for two or three years from 1990 to 1992, where I was really seriously sick with chronic fatigue immune deficiency syndrome (CFIDS). I was 32 at the time. I know a lot of it was due to stress—I'm sure I blew out my adrenal gland: I had a kid, I was trading, I was competing my horse, playing tennis, running, everything under the sun. And of course," she added wryly, gesturing to the huge garden we could see from the window, "keeping up a perfect house and yard and planting all those tulips. I literally got so sick that I could not move off the couch. I had zero energy—I actually had to quit trading for six months. All I could do was sleep all day long. I could not stay awake, I could not get better.

"I went to every doctor—I went to allergy specialists, I had CAT scans, MRIs—my head hurt so badly I was sure I had brain tumors. My glands were always swollen, I couldn't swallow. At night, I would sweat so badly I would have to sleep in a different bed and change T-shirts all night long. It was horrible. I was one of those people who had hardly ever been to a doctor in my entire life—I was the person who was invulnerable to everything, nothing could get me down. I was Ms. Self-Sufficient: I could put myself through school, I could move here or there, I could handle anything! But I couldn't handle it when my own body gave out. It literally collapsed, and I could *not* get better."

Linda looked out the window. "And I remember lying upstairs in the middle of the summer while my husband was outside playing with Erika—I couldn't even take care of my kid—I remember crying, thinking, 'God, just take me now, I just want to die.' But you know, I really didn't feel badly about it. If I hadn't had a kid, I really could have taken my own life—I was that miserable. I thought, if I die right now, it would really, really be okay with me, because I feel like I've done it all. I really have led a great life: I did well, I had fun, I had a chance to train a horse and compete it, I had a chance to do really well in the markets, I met a great man and married him—and I peaked! It can't get any better than it's been. If I have to go, fine.

"When you've gone through that experience, it does make you reevaluate things and reassess your priorities. To tell you the truth, to this day, I still feel like, okay, I did it all by age 32. I peaked. And after that, it didn't really matter so much having things for myself. I just reached the point where I was so grateful that I could walk around the block and have a life again. Now, I feel very responsible for giving to the system, that my life is not my own anymore. I definitely owe everything to a higher life force out there."

For the next few minutes, we talked a little more about more personal things. Many of the women I speak to cite the support and understanding of their spouses as one of the pillars of their success, because it takes an understanding partner to accept the demands the industry puts on a trader. Linda and her husband Skip really seem to function as a team. It might help that Skip was a trader himself and knows what Linda has to put up with.

When I first met my husband, I told Linda, it really helped that he understood the business that I was in, because it's very demanding, as is yours. I don't think most people understand the demands of Wall Street, or of managing money, or of trading. Linda responded, "This business would be too weird for me if I didn't have people around me who understood the business in the sense that the business *is* my life. Ninety-eight percent of the people I know, the friends I have, the people I talk to on the phone—they're all in the markets. I don't know any other normal people out there except the people at the stable, and I don't think I'd call them normal," she said, laughing. "That's my only other outlet, the only other place I know people from. I stay in touch with one childhood girlfriend from high school, and I don't stay in touch with anybody from college. Everybody I know is a trader or in the business."

It seems to be a very difficult business that way, I agreed. It's like you never leave it, it's so much part of your life. "I think in that sense it makes it a little bit more difficult to relate to other people," Linda observed. I think you get a very, very thick skin in this business because there's a lot of things that can go wrong and problems you have to deal with all the time."

Which led to the next area of discussion. I know in the broadcasting business, and Wall Street to a certain extent, that's why people live so hard: A lot of people drink too much or do drugs, because they don't know how to handle the stress. Have you seen much of that? I asked Linda. "In the mid-80s on the floor I'm sure there were the same abuses in any business, be it doctors, attorneys, or anybody who had too much money," Linda responded. "Now, I don't see it. The other CTAs and money managers I see lead very worthy lives: They donate to causes, they have families, they have good values, they try very hard for their clients. You can't survive too long if you're abusing the system. It's going to show up invariably on your bottom line."

Because I know Linda has a seven-year-old daughter (Erika, who sat in on some of our interview, and obviously looks up to her mom), it seemed only natural to ask her how she makes the personal life/career puzzle work. "I'll tell you," Linda said seriously, "there's nothing as much work as taking care of kids. People don't appreciate the incredible amount of work it takes—it's a tremendously stressful thing to do." She was silent for a few seconds before joking, "I guess it helps having only one kid. I don't think I could do three kids and have my business. It wouldn't be fair to the kids. And I'm fortunate that my husband does that stuff—makes sure her lunch is made, does her homework with her every day, and goes to the parent-teachers' meetings. He fulfills that role. If you have a partner in life, it's definitely a team approach, and they can be as big a part of the team even though they're not directly involved in your business, but they make your world go. That's what Skip does in my case."

But you work very hard at trading as well, I noted, so it's a trade-off. "Everything's a trade-off," Linda replied. I *do* work extremely hard. I get up at 5:30, I work out from 6:00 to 7:00, because if I didn't work out my brain wouldn't function during the day, and I'm in my office at 7:30. I'm in here answering phones until around 6:30 P.M., and then I'm usually back in my office at 9:30 at night, doing analysis for the next day. On weekends there's a constant stream of things to get done, so it's really a seven-day-a-week thing. It's not just my business or my work, this is my life, this is what I do. But I also feel like success is not just a function of how hard I work. Even though I work very hard, I probably don't have to work as hard as I do, because the number one key to success is that you have to have that belief, that *vision*. Any dream that you have in your mind—you can make it into a reality."

I told Linda that when both she and John Murphy were doing a segment on CNBC, John had told me Linda was the best trader in the world. I also mentioned he isn't the only person I've heard that from. I asked Linda how she felt about that, and she seemed slightly embarrassed, waving her hand as if to dismiss such praise. "Oh, that's very nice of John to say that. There are some phenomenal people out there who are far better traders than me. I feel like I definitely have the *ability,* in my own mind, to be the best trader in the world. I really do feel like I can be the best, but I don't feel like I *am* now, by any means. Being the best trader in the world has 100 percent to do with your concentration level. And over the last three years I have had to back off a little bit. Building up a business like this takes up so much time and energy, it doesn't allow you to necessarily be the best trader in the world. Probably 60 percent of my energy was initially going to working with people, training them, and setting up my business.

"You have to have that environment where you have 100 percent concentration on the markets. Hopefully, I'm getting back to that now. I do feel like I can do the best analysis in the world, and a lot of times I know very well what's going to happen in a certain market, but people don't realize it's not exclusively about having that knowledge, it's preparing yourself mentally and psychologically to take advantage of it. Because a lot of times it feels very uncomfortable going against a certain grain or being aggressive in an area other people aren't, and you have to get yourself very, very psyched up to do it—you know, who's going to step over that line the first time? Well, the person who does, who takes that first step off the cliff, is ultimately the one who's going to make the most money. You can't make money following the pack, which is the comfortable thing to do. It's that emotional and psychological side you have to get yourself into."

Of all the women I spoke to, Linda was the only one who traded almost exclusively in the futures markets. I wondered if her approach differed significantly from others I'd talked to. Not surprisingly, she's systematic and realistic. "I'm pretty much 100 percent technical analysis," she said, highlighting a trend I've noticed among many women I've talked to lately. "I might look at other things in a very casual way, like market composition—is it 80 percent commercial longs right now, are the small speculators bullish? A lot of it is common sense. I used to thrive a lot more on being a little bit contrarian, but occasionally there are still blatant signals. I remember the bond market a couple of months ago was an obvious sell because I heard all these analysts on TV talking about how you should buy all you could. Any time I hear people making wild, long-term statements, it just sends little antennas up because *nobody* can tell you what's going to happen six months down the road, I don't care if they've got an IQ of 200. It's like trying to tell me in March what the weather is going to be like in August. You simply cannot know all the variables that are going to occur between now and then."

One apparently contrarian aspect of her personality is that while most traders bask in whatever notoriety they get, Linda tends to view that aspect of the business as more of a distraction than anything else. "If I could change anything," she said, laughing somewhat nervously, "I would eliminate all the phone calls and the letters and the faxes, and disruptions, and I would change my name and go underground so I could just do my analysis on the markets in peace."

So journalists like me wouldn't haunt you?

"You asked!" Linda said, laughing. "But I do feel an obligation to respond to people. . . . I've got piles of faxes from people, a lot of cries for help, and it's a big responsibility. I feel more of a responsibility to my clients, to my business and my bottom line. I also have an obligation because I've written a book and I'd be a real jerk if I said, 'Okay, I'll take your money, but I won't help you out.' But I have a time horizon at which point I'm going to cut that off, and it's probably going to be when I move to Florida. I want to spend time with my family, with my daughter while she's growing up—these are precious years. I really feel like I've neglected my husband and my daughter for the last two years. Now is the time when my daughter needs me the most.

"The thing that makes it tolerable for me now is that I know it's not going to last forever. I'm going to change my name, get an unlisted phone number and move offshore or go underground and just concentrate on making money for my clients. I really don't care about people looking at my performance record. We've pretty much been closed for the last two years, we haven't been accepting money—I don't need to grow. I like my business just the size that it is right now."

Before Linda spent all her time in the markets, she spent hours every day at the keyboard, practicing piano and studying music. Although she told me she no longer keeps up her music regimen, and in fact felt liberated when she didn't have to devote so much time to it, I pointed out that she seems to have traded one all-consuming passion for another—playing the markets instead of the piano. She didn't argue.

"Oh, exactly. Instead of sitting down at the piano now, these computers (she gestures towards the monitors in her office) are my keyboard, and I can work them as well as I used to play the piano. My major was composition. I originally wanted to go into film scoring, and I studied very hard at that, writing pieces and arranging music. I was actually very good with the electronic and engineering aspects of it. Now, it's really not that much different, analyzing the markets instead of music, looking for the patterns that reoccur, certain things that repeat themselves.

"When I started playing the piano, I was around five years old, and I practiced every day, all through college, up to six hours a day, and I didn't know any other way of life. It's the same way now, I come in here and work seven days a week—it's just what I do. You just keep on plodding through. But it works—I hope. You have to have that ability to do a lot of work in the meantime without expecting an immediate payoff—and that's true of anything. I'll come in here and I'll grind away day after day without necessarily seeing any monetary reward. You just have to have that belief that, well, a year or so down the road, somehow, it will pay off. There are a lot of days or weeks I don't make money. I think that's probably the most difficult thing for people who start out trading: They feel like they're not a success if they haven't made money in six months, or even a year, and that's not really what the game is about at all. And in our society, we especially want instant gratification, instant satisfaction, instant results. It's like when people go into a weight training program: 'What, I'm not going to see results for six months, why bother?' It's a process, one step at a time."

It was getting late, and I had a long drive home. I said good-bye to everyone and got back on the road as the day's last sunlight was filtering through the trees. I played back some of the interview tapes to make sure the recording went okay. As I listened to Linda's voice, I felt somewhat overwhelmed hearing this woman talk about the step-by-step process of achieving her goals and her single-minded dedication to her work. Make no mistake about it, despite the relaxed atmosphere of the day, Linda is still definitely high-energy, and just listening to her at this late hour was tiring.

Julie Stone

Senior Investment Management Consultant,
Smith Barney

While not necessarily all the "Women of the Street" work in the shadow of the New York Stock Exchange, Aspen, Colorado, surely qualifies as one of the more remote (but glamorous) locations for a financial mover and shaker to hang her shingle. Known internationally as an expensive hideaway for the rich and beautiful, Aspen was first and always a scenic and secluded corner of nature, blessed with gorgeous vistas and ski-friendly mountainsides. Most people go there to "get away," or at least to rub elbows with other jet-setters. But for ace broker Julie Stone, Aspen is a second home, a place where she can do business—and get in a little skiing in season. More than an accomplished downhill skier, though, Julie is a shrewd businesswoman who has successfully navigated more than a few slippery slopes in her career and personal life and has passed on what she has learned to other women in her work as an advocate of women's education and empowerment in the markets.

The Rocky Mountains may *seem* like a million miles from Wall Street, but with today's technology, that's really just an illusion. Julie spends three days a week in Aspen and the rest of her time in Denver. A stockbroker since 1987, she's among the top investment management consultants at Smith Barney. Together with her partner, she has developed a customer base of high net-worth individuals and foundations. Her job: Assist clients with personal investment strategies and match them with the right money managers. Her average customer's portfolio is $550,000, and she and her partner are responsible for over $100 million in total assets.

We met for coffee in a little cafe called the Wienerstube across the street from her Aspen office. We had the place almost to ourselves; in the off-season, Aspen becomes much more small townish and relaxed. I stretched my legs and admired the mountain view out the front window as we waited for our coffee. Having just gotten through with a three-leg flight, I felt rather rumpled next to Julie, who was sporting a full-fledged "Aspen-business" look: perfectly groomed hair, black cowboy hat, suede shirt, charcoal gray skirt, and cowboy boots. Luckily, Julie is one of those people who makes you feel at ease, probably because she's so at ease with herself. Her poise and self-confidence, I would find out, were many years in the making.

Animated and unequivocal, Julie spun one of the more fascinating tales I'd heard, spanning nearly 30 years, three careers, and two marriages. Over the course of her narrative, a picture gradually emerged of an outspoken and original thinker whose will to succeed (and willingness to grow) carried her to the top of her profession.

From an early age, Julie was aware of the social disparities between men and women, specifically, how gender differences typically manifested themselves in money and business issues. The daughter of an entrepreneurial father who controlled the family purse strings, Julie grew up in an era (the '50s and '60s) when women commonly got cash from their husbands to buy the groceries, clothes, and other necessities; Julie's mother, for example, didn't have a checking account, nor was she included on her husband's account. Forced to budget carefully, Julie's mom became "a cash management person," dividing the money into envelopes and designating them for different expenses.

"She would begin to set aside money to buy us dresses for school, putting the clothes on layaway until she gathered enough together," Julie recalled. "Naturally, she became skilled at cash management and passed it on to us. When I grew up, women had very little access to money, and they were too busy raising large families to work outside the home. Women were not able to invest, since all the money given them was earmarked for something essential. Money wasn't around for long, it was spent within the next week, or month, or two months. So cash in hand was very important—it meant survival."

In high school and college, and in her early career, Julie was restricted to a modest allowance or a tight budget. She found herself implementing the very same money-handling techniques, or as she says, honing her skills at stretching money.

"Later, when I was grown and in school or working, I kept cash in different envelopes the same way, and I could tangibly see how much money I had. This established a spending pattern which helped me stay within a very restricted budget: I had an envelope for food and gasoline, an envelope for clothing, an envelope for miscellaneous and entertainment, an envelope for doctor bills and emergencies. If there was something left over in one of the envelopes at the end of the month, I could buy something that was not allotted for. I became experienced at cash management myself—I had an uncanny ability to stretch quarters into dollars."

Julie looked back for a moment on the culture she was raised in, reflecting on how the realities of adulthood often bump up against the expectations of youth. "I was like a lot of women in my generation," she said. "I believed I was going to grow up and marry a man who would take care of me for the rest of my life. I would live happily and protected, the way my father protected me. No one gave me a hint that anything other than good would happen to me, and I had no fears about money. It was simple: A woman's primary job was to find the right protector. My fears associated with money came *later* in life. After two failed marriages, I discovered that Mr. Right also had a flip side—Mr. Wrong—and it suddenly became evident that I could not count on someone else to provide for me. I would have to learn about money and investing to protect myself." Julie stopped for a moment and shook her head. "My God, that sounds healthy now," she noted, "but it was a terrifying realization then."

Long before that realization, however, Julie did meet one woman who represented the possibility of a different kind of life: an uncommonly (for the time) entrepreneurial women who owned the apartment complex Julie lived in as a teenager. "It was the first time I met a female who was responsible for handling all her own finances," Julie remembered. "I was 17 at the time. She would tell a friend of mine and I that we should go to college and then travel— see the world and broaden our experiences—before getting seriously involved with a man. She *also* said we should own our own real estate, which was a new message for me. I began to feel strongly that I wanted to be in charge of my own life and work to make my own money."

She went to college, but things became a little complicated. An early marriage, baby (a "beautiful daughter," now grown), and a quick divorce after two years of school put a tremendous spin on Julie's world, setting off a series of subsequent events that profoundly changed her life. As a single mother with little money, she discovered something unique when she applied for a student loan to complete her education.

"I talked to an older woman in the finance office, and when she found out I had a child, she told me that I should be at home raising my daughter. She would *not* give me a loan. But I was determined, so I searched out her counterpart and told him that I was 23 years old and two years away from completing college. I *also* told him the other loan officer said I should be home raising my daughter. I said, 'Being a single parent will be very difficult for me unless I have an education. How am I going to raise and educate a child if I can't complete college?' He conceded the point and gave me the loan for $1,000. This was the first time I felt that the glass ceiling above my head was controlled by women as well as men, and that the way out was sometimes through men, not women."

That's a pretty powerful statement, I thought, and certainly one you don't hear many women express—at least publicly. I was quickly learning, however, that Julie is a woman who thinks for herself and isn't afraid to voice those thoughts.

But her battles against entrenched attitudes were just beginning. After getting her B.A., she worked as an educator in San Bernadino Valley Community College in California. Although she worked for a very sympathetic, kind-hearted male supervisor, Julie experienced the salary discrepancies with which women are all too commonly confronted in the work world. Typically, Julie met the challenge head on.

"I noticed that one of the men in the program, who was not very effective, was being paid more than I was," remembered Julie. "I would leave my boss newspapers articles describing how women were typically not paid as much as men, and so on. After he read them he would say, 'Thank you, Julie, for letting me read this,' and put them back in my box. Eventually, that male colleague left the program, but I still never got paid the money he made when I assumed his responsibilities. But by this time I was in total control of my own money—I even had a retirement program. I found I was very good at handling money."

A second marriage led to a relocation to Denver, where real estate was booming. Answering a newspaper ad, Julie embarked on a new career as a real estate broker. Things began happening quickly. "Sometimes I would make $8,000 a month, which was serious money in 1970," Julie said. "I decided to continue doing that since there seemed to be no ceiling on what I could make." Julie smiled. "I developed quite a fortune selling land, buying houses, duplexes, apartments, and renovating them, but I wanted to have my own real estate company."

Together with two real estate colleagues, she did just that—and the company took off. "I never really needed household money again," Julie said, providing an idea of just how well things "took off." "I enjoyed business and I enjoyed working for myself—there were no limits. I could make as much as anyone, as long as I worked as hard. In fact, our top agents were all women." Julie was silent for a moment. "But unfortunately," she continued, "the ceiling over my head took on a new form."

The source of the problem was a surprising one: As Julie became more successful in her career, her second marriage unraveled. Although she was bringing in the lion's share of the couple's income and made all the material decisions regarding the real estate business, her husband handled the finances, and troubles arose when she tried to assert some control over the situation. The problem continued to fester, to the point that the couple eventually sought outside help.

Julie described the situation at the time. "At first, all of our marital money went into a joint checking account from which we took care of our houses and bought more real estate. When it got to the point where I was writing 70 or 80 checks a month, it became unbearable for my husband to balance the checkbook. We went to see a counselor, who suggested that money for the household go into a separate checking account to pays for things like food, clothing, vacations, etc." Julie's eyes widened as she recalled the realization of what had happened. "These were the very same things my mother had been in charge of 30 years ago! How ironic that even though I made more money than my husband, I was reliving my mother's role."

Julie leaned forward as she tried to explain how she felt. "My goal was to make a lot of money so we could retire in our 40s—that's what I was working for. I also wanted to create wealth under my own name, but my husband apparently perceived this as a loss of control. I suffered a new inner conflict; it seemed to me then that money generated problems when I wanted to decide how to spend it. Our marriage ended in divorce."

Julie had something of an insight regarding her professional drive while skiing, of all things. "I had a fear of heights when I first learned to ski," she recalled. "I was able to overcome this by not looking way down the mountain. Instead I just looked 10 feet in front while skiing—this became my way of overcoming my fear of heights. I saw parallels in other areas of my life. Making money was a way of overcoming my fear of future poverty. I believe that many women, whether they have money or not, have an underlying fear that they will end up on the streets alone as a bag lady. Consequently, some women tend to hold onto their money much more than men and often don't take risks with investments."

Another shift in the economic landscape ushered in the next phase of Julie's life—and another forum in which she could further explore her money issues. When the tax reform act of 1986 diminished the advantages of owning real estate, Julie liquidated her holdings, believing that the only place money could flow was to stocks and bonds. Considering this development an opportunity rather than a calamity, Julie decided to switch careers: She sold off her business, studied for the securities exam, and got a job with a New York investment firm. She found the investment possibilities of this new world fascinating and was intrigued by its differences from the career she had just left.

"Stocks and bonds were totally different for me," Julie conceded, "and a new way for me to overcome my fear with money. They are intangible assets compared to real estate—you can see real estate, you can drive by it. The value of stocks and bonds moved up and down more rapidly during any given week or month or year than the values of real estate, which seemed to be a much more comfortable asset to own. My perception of what was safe, however, was just that—a perception—it was not necessarily true or valid. I realized I had to change this perception in order to become more comfortable handling stocks and bonds."

Judging by her subsequent performance, Julie's adjustment has been a success. Her personal journey has also resulted in her rounded and insightful perspective on finance, which helps her communicate investment facts with other women facing some of the same issues she has in the past.

Six years ago Julie teamed up with a partner whose primary residence was Aspen. Julie began teaching investment classes at a local junior college and, together with her partner, brought a new level of investment consulting services to the area. She also writes for the local paper.

In Denver, Julie organizes investment seminars and workshops in cooperation with CPAs, women's groups, the chamber of commerce, banking institutions, and attorneys. Speaking, educating, consulting, networking and synergizing have moved her to the top of her profession.

"Many clients are afraid of something that has moving parts that they can't possibly control," Julie explained. "None of us can control the stock market, the bond market, interest rate movements, the economy, the trade deficit. All we can control is our *own* risk level. Depending on how scared or brave we are, our particular risk level is lower or higher. If we are willing to accept only a very low risk level, we may end up making less money and accumulating less wealth; if we can handle a higher risk level, we are able to accumulate more wealth. I became committed to finding a process that would help others learn how to manage their money in a more comfortable way.

"Some women will hesitate to put what they've learned into practice—unless they can move beyond the paralysis engendered by fear. I understand the problem many women face because I've experienced many of the same fears myself. In some areas, I realized that in order to get women to invest, there would have to be a way of reducing the complexity of information and making the process more understandable so they could come to a decision—and get on with investing." She saw her business and educational experiences as the perfect skills for her new career.

Julie initially worked as a stockbroker for approximately six months, and she herself felt the impact of the amount of information required in investing. "I remember feeling overwhelmed by the sheer immensity of the information out there—on top of the fact that it changes every day. You can't just learn it once and be done with it. The information is a moving target. The things you can rely on are the investment process itself, developing a plan, and staying in the process long-term."

The problem can be compounded by the fact that no one on Wall Street can give you the ins and outs of the investment world: Julie had to find out the hard way, through experience. "When I first entered the securities world, I looked for something I could understand well in a short period of time so I could get on the phone and start selling. I was encouraged to get on the phone and tell a convincing story so that people would be inspired to buy on that story. I was uncomfortable with that. It was hard for me to sell something that I did not thoroughly believe in.

"But therein lies my female strength and weakness. I didn't feel I had enough information, I didn't feel comfortable telling a story I didn't believe in; if I wasn't convinced myself, how could I sell to someone else? One day, General Electric's earnings are fine. A day later, two weeks later, they're not because something has changed. I needed a lot of questions answered before I could feel comfortable. This sense of being uncomfortable because of the lack of a complete understanding is what keeps many people from investing."

But it didn't take her long to find her niche—"investment management consulting"—even with the challenges of her new field. "My job is to identify managers in the top percentile who fit the asset class requirements of a client. You can create solid asset allocation and investment-style diversification that allows a client to be a very comfortable long-term investor, and long-term is where the potential reward of wealth resides."

Not surprisingly, Julie believes that men and women relate to risk differently. "Men and women often carry absolutely opposite views. I've noticed that men move more quickly into higher risk areas. For men and women to survive, they have to make money to support their families, and they are more highly motivated to continue to move up the ladder from one car to another car, from one house to another house, from one level of wealth to a higher level of wealth. Men, I believe—more than women—really buy into the perception that they need to be worth more all the time. So in order to achieve this, they take more risks.

"Traditionally," Julie continued, "many women felt they wouldn't *survive* if they took risks. When I started out, I found I was analyzing a lot of miscellaneous information and didn't have a process by which to filter and clarify it all in order to make an informed decision. It resulted in an impasse for me; however, for men, information often seems to just fall out of the funnel into a decision. But now I find that women, especially, once they get going, there's no stopping them. I'm the one counseling that they slow down or be more conservative."

Abruptly, Julie stood up, turned, and asked me, "Do *you* think men have a different approach to investing?" I hesitated. "I think men believe they're responsible for solving problems," I said finally. "Typically if you ask a man for his help, he goes directly into action mode. Perhaps you just want him to listen to you, to bounce the problem around a little, but he usually responds with a directive."

"That's true," Julie agreed. "Many men will immediately try to solve the problem and present a solution—not so much empowering you as an equal, but rather telling you what to do as an expert. Men, by taking over the problem in order to solve it, *can* reduce the esteem of a female client without meaning to, which can be demeaning if she hasn't been listened to appropriately. She feels fear, then retreats."

I wanted to draw Julie out on this subject a little more, so I asked her if she thinks women make better financial advisors than men. "Women brokers listen for the emotional tone and address it," she replied. "Men usually don't hear the emotional side clearly and just breeze over it, with the result that a woman feels left out of the decision-making process. I can't count the times I've heard women say how their fathers, bankers, brokers, husbands, uncles—whichever man is helping them with their financial decisions—just take over and exclude them. I tell women to ask for what they really need—to be heard and included in the decision-making process. When a woman is active in making the decision, it's hers. She can now trust the process because she understands it. Convincing is never as effective for a woman as explaining."

Jabbing a pen in the air to accentuate her points, Julie summed up a critical difference between many male and female brokers: "When a woman comes to a male broker or consultant for help, the male hears, 'I want your help, I can't solve the problem. Will you solve it for me?' The female broker or consultant might hear the same client differently: 'I don't know how to solve this problem. Will you listen to me, and help me solve the problem?'

Like other notable female financial pros, Julie believes the investment world is a relationship business: She makes a living matching people up and developing investment strategies, and she has found women possess natural attributes that can actually help them excel in this male-dominated field. "I've found ongoing relationships and friendships," Julie said of her own career. "That certainly makes being in the securities world a lot more fulfilling. This approach allows me not only to bring in all the skills I've learned throughout my life, but also to use all my natural feminine characteristics: intuition, a willingness to listen, an inclination to be caring and compassionate, an ability to communicate complex concepts in a simple way, and the skill of demonstrating the fundamental mechanisms by which it all works. When I can show others how to use their own innate qualities, they immediately become very powerful and skillful investors."

The process can sometimes be an uphill battle, though. "I have found over and over again that people want to make 12 to 15 percent average on their money every year, with no down years. The minute their account is flat—it's not making as much as a CD rate, for instance—they begin to get nervous. The fact is, all investments go through down periods, and you have to keep the long haul in mind. I inform my clients about what to realistically expect. Information, process, patience—it takes all three to develop wealth."

The changing demographics of our society make the need for women to understand and take charge of their investments more imperative than ever. "A female now has a greater chance of outliving the money that has been saved by her husband or jointly. Men also need to be actively involved in drawing their wives or female partners into the investment process."

Julie's advice to female investors: "Pursue balance in your investing as you do in other areas of your lives. Women have been practicing balance their whole lives. They simply need to engage the skills they already have in developing an investment portfolio and plan, then persist in staying with the plan long-term."

According to Julie, this can and should be more of a natural process. "Even though women already inherently know how to do it, 'investing' often feels foreign to them. Men, on the other hand, zero in on something, buy it, and they're in. What's so ironic is that anyone can absolutely handle the complexity of investing once they understand what they can and cannot control."

It's not a matter of needing different, or better, skills according to Julie; it's all about mastering a process. "I believe that women, more than men, talk about things between themselves, and explore all the aspects of a situation. Women are extremely well positioned to become successful investors—having already acquired many of the skills, having the background and the talent, and being focused on achieving balance. Women often simply need to get a handle on a process by which to develop a long-term investment plan and make the hard decisions. Getting hold of these tools can dissolve a woman's fears.

"Men traditionally get their power from being in charge of money. Often, women don't move fast enough to catch the opportunity. Men want to actively make money; they forge ahead. If it doesn't work, it doesn't work: They just go at it again. Men freely tell stories about their mistakes and losing 'the big one.' Women tend to beat themselves up badly if their stocks go down."

Julie, of course, thinks there needs to be more equilibrium in the male and female approaches to investing. And as much as she teaches other people, she still learns from her own clients. The inexorable march of the baby boomers toward retirement provided one important lesson. "The female approach is more of what baby boomer clients want, both male and female," said Julie. "They want to be involved, to understand the process, to put it on their PCs at home. This might result in a better balance between how men and women approach investing, and how male and female brokers and consultants handle their clients. There's an evolution underway that I think will produce much better investors. Meanwhile, though, we can't wait for the end results of this evolution, we've got to do the work now."

Without a doubt, Julie Stone is doing her part. And the message of education, empowerment, and courage that she embodies for women in the investment world may be a ripple on the pond that leads to another ripple and then another. Who knows, with a few more years and a few more Julie Stones, envelopes may be just for sending letters.

AFTERWORD

No single book can say everything that needs to be said—on any subject. Like the markets themselves, the "story" told by the interviews collected here is constantly unfolding and evolving; the twists and turns it will take are (almost) anyone's guess. Women will certainly still flock to Wall Street, confront obstacles, and continue to transform the face of the financial industry—the work the women in these pages began will be carried on by a new generation.

I wish I could have talked to more women. Many labor behind the scenes in administrative or back-office positions, and in terms of the number of people they manage or the influence they exert on their firms' operations, they undeniably wield a great deal of clout. But the women on the front lines—the traders, analysts, and advisors who are the "face" of the industry—are the ones most *visibly* impacting the Street. For better or worse, these are the personalities the public knows and associates with the fascinating and complex machinations that comprise the investing and trading industry. Unfortunately, some highly placed women, because of career considerations, timing, or personal reasons, decided not to participate. Before too long, hopefully we will have the opportunity to hear their stories as well—underscoring that the experiences and accomplishments of the women in this book are not an aberration, but evidence of the emergence of an influential and pervasive force in the financial industry.

And in the years to come, we can expect to hear the stories of a new generation of female financial professionals for whom the Women of the Street were role models and heroes. More can be said, and should be said, about the challenges women face in the work world in general, and on the Street in particular.

Recent articles in the *New York Times* and *Fortune* magazine dissecting the lives and character traits of high-powered businesswomen suggest these things will indeed come to pass. Many of the themes running through *Women of the Street*—independence, take-it-on-the-chin stoicism, and an insistence on asserting, rather than denying, gender—were in evidence in these articles as well. We have evidently only begun to scratch the surface of this topic.

In the weeks since I wrapped up these interviews, the market has gone on something of a wild ride. Following the amazing rally of 1995, the stock market surged slightly higher in the spring of 1996, only to suffer an unsettling correction in July that had many investors (*and* analysts *and* traders) wondering whether the bull had run its course. Was a bear—or a crash—lurking around the corner? The financial press reported every twist and turn, alternately speculating on doom and preaching calm.

Some of the subjects of this book have fared better than others—and more than one of them has been "in the news" over the past several months—but all of them are still in the game. Given their track records and their collective emphasis on long-term performance, you would hardly expect them to be rattled by a rough patch in the markets. Unlike the most recent crop of hotshot 29-year-old fund managers who've never experienced a bear market (and who were in school when the market crashed in 1987), these women have all seen much worse, and they've all survived—more accurately, they've prospered.

This isn't surprising. If there was any "message" that jumped out from these interviews, it was that women are not only capable of prospering on the Street, they are uniquely suited to success there.

When these women first burst into the Wall Street party, they were basically asked to serve the punch, smile politely, and speak when spoken to. Most men figured they could do little else. The issue, time has shown, was never if they could actually hack it in a man's world, but if they would be given the opportunity—as a group, and on an individual basis. And although one would think that the barriers and prejudices have been knocked down once and for all, every woman finds herself, to one degree or another, having to fight the same battles with one or two (or three) skeptical colleagues or clients to earn respect and get ahead.

Old habits die hard. As much as we'd like to think otherwise, the world has not been completely revolutionized over the last three decades. Yes, substantial gains have been made, but overall, progress has been incremental in many areas, and has been accompanied by a high price tag: stress, divorce, and sacrifices in family time. The rewards are there, but the risks are equally notable. It's been a "two steps forward, one step back" kind of process. Most likely, it will continue that way for a long time. There are, after all, still only two female chief executives in the *Fortune* 500.

But Wall Street is a good barometer for the general progress of women in the workplace. If it appears from these women's stories that some of the major issues have not yet been resolved, or that there is a measure of ambivalence toward the price of success and the impact of discrimination, it is probably because these women are the ones that are making new rules and setting new benchmarks. They're exploring uncharted territory, and if the course is not always sure, the final destination appears somewhat inevitable.

For all the strides women have made, the conflict of raising a family and maintaining a career still seems to present an insoluble problem. Although many of the women in this book have children, the choices they faced were never easy. Employers today are more willing to accommodate the demands of motherhood, but an underlying prejudice still persists in many offices that women are likely to leave a job to have children. Even women who have worked a number of years are suspected of being gone for good when they take off for maternity leave.

Our society, for the most part, seems to have conceded that women can and should be allowed to pursue career ambitions—as long as they still fulfill the traditional domestic roles of homemaker and caretaker. Rather than finding they can "have it all," as the cliché goes, women may find they are forced to "do it all," and suffer the consequences. Interestingly, when men assume any of the traditional homemaking duties, it's still seen as something exceptional; with women, it's still expected. Many women have simply discovered that making time for family means asserting a degree of independence from the office—at whatever cost that decision entails.

While more women than ever are outearning their spouses, it's a development about which our society remains at best, ambivalent, and at worst, downright hostile. Certainly many men, even those who in theory say they have nothing against it, find the situation uncomfortable in practice. As we've seen in these pages, what might be welcomed as an economic bonus to a couple's finances can instead become a source of resentment and competition—an impediment to a happy family life.

Another layer of irony is the guilt and pressure women feel who decide to raise a family rather than work, or who *do* decide to leave their jobs at some point to have children. Rather than being seen as sacrificing the rewards of a career to enjoy the rewards of family life, they are instead viewed by traditional corporate culture (including some women) as traitors to the company, and evidence that women aren't as good a bet as men as long-term employees: "See, they do bail out eventually to have children. Why hire them in the first place?" These are the narrow straits women must navigate.

Why has Wall Street, formerly the ultimate men's club, proved to be such fertile ground for ambitious, talented women who seek an arena with no limits? Whereas there may be more in-your-face testosterone in the financial industry than in others, the entrepreneurial side of the business and its emphasis on bottom-line performance perhaps allows women more opportunity to pursue their dreams without restriction, compared to the more rigid hierarchies (or serendipitous office politics) that prevail in traditional corporate cultures. Although the obstacles are still there on the Street, at least they are clearly visible—out in the open, where you can see them and deal with them.

The future belongs to those women brave enough to flout convention and creative enough to invent their own rules for themselves. That is just what these women have done: They didn't let snubs or slights deter them, they didn't let occasional failures stop them, they didn't accept the labels that were applied to them. Rather than trying to "become" men, they never denied their femininity, and in fact used it to its greatest advantage. Opportunity is self-created on Wall Street, and the Women of the Street are living proof that rules can, should, and always will be broken and remade.

INDEX